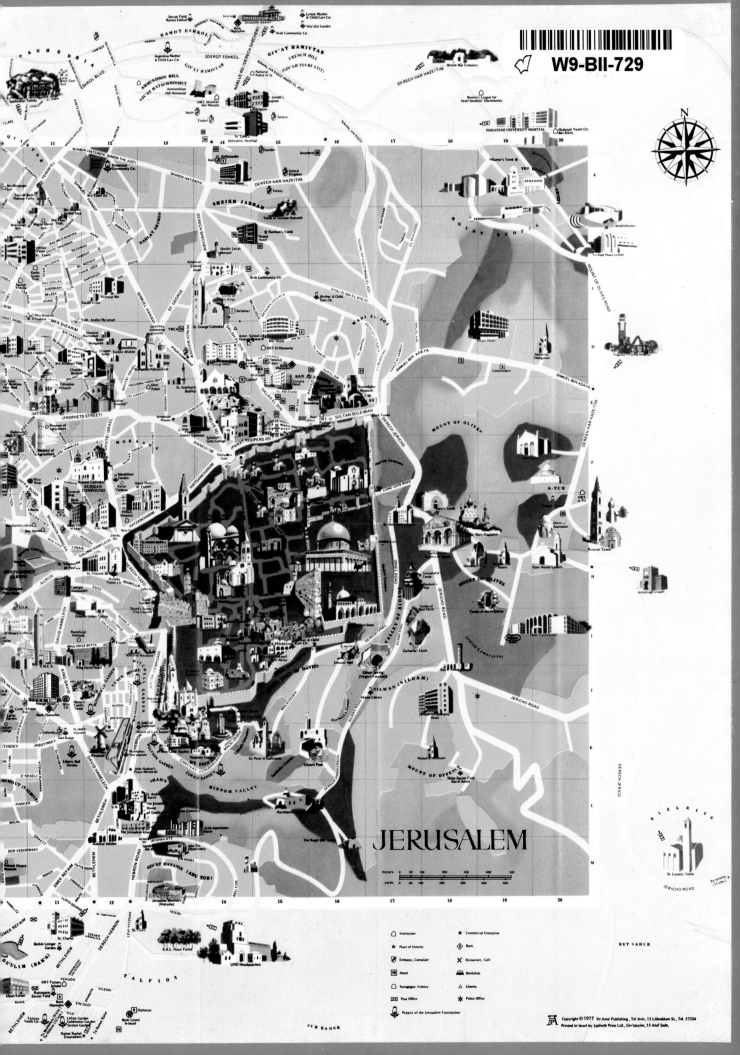

JERUSALEM

HIGHSMITH #45230

Printed
In USA

The glory of Jerusalem

The glory

Cambridge University Press

Cambridge
London   New York   New Rochelle
Melbourne   Sydney

# of Jerusalem

Shlomo S. Gafni
Text

A. van der Heyden
Photography

Acknowledgements

The publishers, author and photographer wish to express their sincere gratitude to the following persons for their help: Bishop Vasilius, Archimandrite Daniel and Mr Anastasios Tsolakis of the Greek Orthodox Patriarchate in Jerusalem; Archimandrite Anthony Grabbe of the Russian Ecclesiastical Mission in Jerusalem; Col. O. Dobbie, Custodian of the Garden Tomb; Father M. Piccirilo of the Studium Biblium Franciscanum; Sister Purdy Donna of the Ecce Homo Convent; Messrs Salah Jarallah and Muhammed Kashur of the Jerusalem Municipality; Mr I. Lippel, Director General, and Dr S.Z. Kahana of the Ministry of Religious Affairs; Mr George Hintlian of the Armenian Patriarchate in Jerusalem; Mr Yosef Aviram of the Israel Exploration Society; Rivka Gonen, M.A.; architects Yitzhak Ephroni and Dror Harouvi and, last but not least, Mrs Rachel Gillon and Miss Hannah Dahan of the Jerusalem Publishing House, for devoted labour in the preparation of this volume.

We thank the following institutions for allowing us to use photographs from their archives: The Israel Exploration Society (pic. 50, 51, 52, 53, 55) and the Department of Antiquities and Museums of the Ministry of Education and Culture (pic. 339). Also the photographers: David Harris (pic. 54, 344); Aliza Auerbach (pic. 185, 192, 193, 194, 196); Rolf Kneller (page 5) and Avinoam Glick (pic. 50, 52, 55).

We thank the management of the Holy Land Hotel in Jerusalem for permission to photograph the model of the City and the Temple Mount in the Second Temple era (pic. 344, 345, 346, 347, 348).

The photographs 261, 262 were taken with the permission and agreement of the Orthodox Palestine Society and the Russian Ecclesiastical Mission in Jerusalem, which is under the Synod of Bishops of the Russian Church Outside Russia, which reserve all rights to them.

We thank the Amir Publishing Company Ltd., Givataim, for giving the permission of reproducing the Jerusalem map.

Research: SHLOMO MARGALIT

English Version: YAEL GUILADI

Language Editor: YAEL LOTAN

Supplementary Photography: ZEV RADOVAN

Published by the Press Syndicate of the University of Cambridge
The Pitt Building, Trumpington Street, Cambridge CB2 1RP
32 East 57th Street, New York, NY 10022, USA
296 Beaconsfield Parade, Middle Park, Melbourne 3206, Australia

© Cambridge University Press 1982

Library of Congress Catalogue number : 81-17053

Printed in Belgium by Offset Printing Van den Bossche

ISBN 0 521 24613X

Contents

Page 4. An aerial view of the Temple Mount. The new excavations beside the western and southern walls are in the foreground.
Page 6. The Kidron Valley with the Tomb of Absalom in the foreground and the village of Siloam in the background. The village is on the site of an ancient Israelite necropolis from the First Temple period.

Introduction

Jerusalem, the Holy City, occupies a special place in the hearts of people throughout the world. Momentous events that took place here shaped the basis for Western civilization. It was here that the foundations were laid for the monotheistic belief, in Judaism and subsequently Christianity and Islam.

This city of King David the warrior-poet, King Solomon the Wise, the Prophets, the Maccabees, John the Baptist and Jesus, often appears more a spiritual symbol than a place where people have lived and toiled for centuries. For Jews everywhere the prayer, "Next year in Jerusalem" repeated each and every day, had been engraved on their consciousness. The Christians were so captivated by the biblical image of Jerusalem that the Crusaders tried to take it in the manner of Joshua — marching around it seven times blowing trumpets . . .

It is difficult to think of Jerusalem as merely a city of the present. The least mystically-inclined visitor cannot help but feel a thrill as he looks over the hills of Judaea, or as he walks through the narrow winding streets of the Old City, with its dramatic historical associations.

Four thousand years ago, Jerusalem was a minor Canaanite kingdom called Iru-Shalim, probably meaning, "Founded by [the God] Shalim." It was situated on the spur and slope south of what is today the Old City, between the Kidron Valley to the east and a smaller cleft to the west. Though defensible, the location did not favour development, for the land was rocky, there were few springs and little rainfall. It began to grow when it became the capital city of the Jewish Kingdom under David, three thousand years ago. His son Solomon built the First Temple and made Jerusalem an important religious and political centre of a relatively powerful kingdom. The prophets Isaiah and Jeremiah then made the city the moral and spiritual centre of our Western world.

Jerusalem's ancient history is minutely documented: King Solomon's Temple and palace are detailed in Kings 6–7 and II Chronicles 3–4. After the return of the Babylonian exiles, its governor Nehemiah left an account of its condition and his plans for repairs and restoration. After the destruction of the Second Temple in 70 A.D., the Jewish historian Josephus Flavius wrote a faithful and detailed description of the Temple Mount, the upper city and the royal palaces. His account is complemented in the Talmud, in tractates *Midot* (measurements) and *Qorban* (sacrifice).

After Constantine made Christianity the official religion of the Roman Empire, Jerusalem became the focus of Christian pilgrimage. Beginning with the itinerary of an anonymous pilgrim who, in 333, journeyed from Bordeaux to Jerusalem, a vast amount of such literature has accumulated, including the writings of prominent historical figures, such as Theodosius and Antonius of Placentia in the 6th century, Arculfus in the 8th, Felix Fabri in the 15th, and Quaresmius in the 17th century. Their descriptions of the Holy City provide a wealth of invaluable information.

To this day, Jerusalem is not only an encapsulated history of the Middle East and the Western world, it is also — for Jews, for Christians and for Moslems — an embodiment of religious faith, a lodestone for pilgrimage, a symbol of spiritual glory. At the same time, it is an earthly city, very much alive, developing and thriving. Its past and present merge before our eyes as we look to its future.

Teddy Kollek

1

2

Jerusalem has never ceased to hold a mystical fascination for mankind. Spread out gracefully upon the crest of the Judaean hills which divide the desert from the sea, it has always stood aloof from the hustle and bustle of the main thoroughfares through the Holy Land. Yet all those who down the ages sought to contemplate its beauty, made the ascent not wearily but with joy. Millions have trodden the paths, the steps, the roads and the highways which make their way round Judaea's gentle slopes, winding through its enchanting landscape of richest gold and green, up to the eternal city.

Since ancient times, the main route to Jerusalem from the Mediterranean coast led across the Ayalon Valley and, by way of Latrun, to Maaleh Beit Horon and to Sha'ar Hagai, gateways to the gorge which climbs to the city. The Crusader fortress at Latrun, placed strategically where the valley runs into the Judaean foothills (1), commands a breathtaking panorama of the approaches to Jerusalem from the sea. Inevitably, its surroundings have been the scene of the countless battles fought through the centuries to gain control of Jerusalem: Joshua with Canaanites, Maccabees with Greeks, Romans with Jews, Arabs with Byzantines, Moslems with Crusaders, Israelis with Arabs. But today the main Jerusalem—Tel-Aviv highway runs through Emek Ayalon, a black ribbon through the golden wheat fields.

In due time, modern civilisation came to the ancient city. In 1892 one of the first railway lines to be constructed in the Middle East was built to link Jerusalem with the Mediterranean port of Jaffa (2). It was widened by the British during the First World War, and a station was built to serve the Arab villages of the surroundings. Though the station no longer functions, the railway still meanders leisurely through the terraced hillsides of Judaea.

The remains of the Roman road from Motza to Jerusalem (3) would seem to be a continuation of the route which led through Emmaus — the Greek name for Latrun — to Sha'ar Hagai. Motza is mentioned in early Jewish writings, and recent excavations have revealed traces of Roman and Byzantine settlement there. Indeed, Roman documents indicate that on the site, referred to by its Latin name Colonia, stood a village for veteran legionaries, founded by Vespasian. In places, the present road follows the delightful, tree-lined Roman route.

The Roman road from the sea coast led up to Jerusalem by way of the steep slope of Beit Horon (4). These steps were hewn out of the bedrock, but archaeologists are not certain whether they served as a support for a road which was laid upon them, or whether were used as we can see them today. The work was carried out in the second century A.D., perhaps by order of the Emperor Hadrian.

1. A view from the Crusader fortress of Latrun over the road leading to Jerusalem.
2. The railroad line from Jaffa to Jerusalem, winding uphill through the Nahal Sorek Valley.
3. The Roman road to Jerusalem which ran through Motza — a delightful tree-lined route.
4. Near Beit Horon, the Roman road was hewn out of the bedrock.

3

4

Beit Horon is mentioned in many ancient chronicles, for battle after battle was fought there for control over the access to the city. Here Saul and David confronted the Philistines, Judah Maccabee defeated the Greeks, and a Jewish force defeated the Roman governor Cestius Gallus at Beit Horon.

Gentler are the steps which led up north-eastwards through the Elah Valley from Beit Guvrin (5). They were probably built about the same time as those of Beit Horon and, like them, were the scene of endless struggles between Jerusalem's successive conquerors. This was the site of David's legendary combat with Goliath. Thereafter, there were two more battles which David fought against the Philistines along this ancient route, as described in the Book of Samuel, and Nebuchadnezzar may have passed this way when he captured Judaea and Jerusalem.

During the Roman occupation, the Bet Guvrin road was one of the main routes from the coast to Jerusalem. Josephus and Pliny make frequent mention of villages which lay along it. Roman milestones have been discovered along this route indicating the distance from Jerusalem, or Aelia Capitolina as the Romans called it, to Bet Guvrin.

The Romans usually set not one, but a group of stones (6) to mark their mile, a unit which was equivalent to a thousand double paces — *milia passuum* — hence its name. The first stone served as a commemorative plaque to mark the construction of the road, while the others gave details of repairs and improvements to it. The stones found on the Beit Guvrin road are of local limestone. Between 150 and 250 centimetres high, their form is identical: a square base on which rests a cylindrical stone, whose upper edge is sometimes decorated with a cornice.

The inscriptions engraved on the cylindrical stones were usually composed of two distinct parts: the official Latin text dedicated to the emperor in whose reign the road was built; and the informative section indicating the distance from the main city where the road began and, sometimes, from the locality to which it led. During Hadrian's rule this text was written for the first time in the Greek vernacular, a practice which became universally accepted under Marcus Aurelius.

The Roman milestones were a powerful means of propaganda, much as the giant hoardings placed along our modern highways are today. By reminding the traveller with mathematical precision at every one of the thirty miles along the Jerusalem—Beit Guvrin road of the great achievements of its emperors, Rome created in the minds of the people it had subjected an impression of immutable might which no power could ever challenge.

5. The rock-hewn Roman road which ran through the Elah valley, connecting Jerusalem with Bet Guvrin and Gaza.
6. Roman milestones discovered along the Roman road from Jerusalem to Bet Guvrin. The stones were not all found exactly where they stand today, but in the immediate vicinity.
7. Close-up of a Roman milestone.

[IMP(erator) CAES(ar) M(arcus) AUREL(ius) ANTONINUS]
[AUG(ustus) PONT(ifex) MAX(imus) TRIB(unicia) POTEST(ate) XVI (?)]
[CO(n)S(ul) III (?) ET IMP(erator) CAES(ar) L(ucius) AUREL(ius)]
(VERUS TRIB(unicia) POTEST(ate) II (?) CO(n)S(ul) II (?)]
[DIVI] ANTON[INI FILI(i) DI] VI
HADRIANI NEP[OTES DIVI]
TRAIANI PARTH[ICI] PRONEP[OTES]
DIVI NERVAE [A] BNEP(otes) M(ilia)
    [P(assuum) XX] VI
[A]ΠΟ ΚΟΛ(ωνίας) ΑΙΛ(ίας) [ΚΑΠ(ιπωλίνας) (?) ΜΙΛΙΑ ΚΔ]

The Emperor Caesar Marcus Aurelius Antoninus
Augustus Supreme Pontiff Sixteenth-time Tribune (?)
Third-time Consul (?) And the Emperor Caesar Lucius Aurelius
Verus Second-time Tribune Second-time Consul
Sons of the Divine Antoninus Grandsons of the Divine Hadrian
Great-grandsons of the Divine Trajan Conqueror of the Parthians
Great-great-grandsons of the Divine Nerva (2)6 miles   *(should be 24)*
From the Colony Aelia Capitolina 24 Miles

IMP(eratori) CAES(ari) L(ucio) SEPTI(mio)
SEVERO PIO PERTI
NACI AUG(usto) ARAB(ico)
ADIAB(enico) PART(hico) MAX(imo)
TRIB(unicia) POTES(tate) XI IMP(eratori) VII
CO(n)S(uli) II
IMP(eratori) CAES(ari) M(arco) AUREL(io)
ANTONINO AUG(usto) [[[L(ucio) SEPT(imio)]]]
[[[GETAE NOBIL(issimo)]]]
[[[CAES(ari)]]] ANTONINI
AUG {G} (usti) N(ostri) [[[FRATRI (?)]]]
[ΑΠΟ ΚΟΛ(ωνίας) ΑΙΛΙΑΣ ΚΑΠ(ιπωλίνας) (?)
      ΜΕΙΛΙΑ
      ΚΔ

To the Emperor Caesar Lucius Septimius
Severus the Pious Pertinax Augustus Conqueror of the Arabs Conqueror of
Adiabene Greatest Conqueror of the Parthians
Eleventh-time Tribune   *(should be seventh)*
Seventh-time Emperor *(should be eleventh)*
Second-time Consul
And the Emperor Caesar Marcus Aurelius **Antoninus Augustus and Lucius Septimius** Geta Caesar the
Noblest Brother of Antoninus our Augustus
From Colony Aelia Capitolina (?) Miles 24

8

9

10

On the ancient road which leads westward from Jericho (8), winding through the Judaean wilderness up to the Mount of Olives, lies the delightful copse of Beth-Phage. The route, almost certainly built by Hadrian, probably followed an even earlier one. So called after the Aramaic name, *pagi*, for the young figs which grow in profusion nearby, Beth-Phage is closely associated with the last days of Jesus, as they are related in the Gospel according to St. Matthew, 21:1—5: "And when they drew nigh unto Jerusalem, and were come to Beth-Phage, unto the Mount of Olives, then sent Jesus two disciples, saying unto them, 'Go into the village over against you, and straightway ye shall find an ass tied, and a colt with her: loose them and bring them unto me.' ... that it might be fulfilled which was spoken by the prophet saying, 'Tell ye, the daughter of Zion, behold, the King cometh unto thee, meek, and sitting upon an ass, and a colt, the foal of an ass.' "

The newly built road (9) which connects Mount Zion with the Garden of Gethsemane passes alongside the archaeological digs at present being carried out south of the Temple Mount. Since 1967, three thousand years of history have been unearthed on this site, revealing vestiges of no less than five civilisations: Israelite Iron Age burial caves; richly paved streets which were part of Herod's magnificent Second Temple complex; vestiges of the Roman Tenth Legion's encampment; exquisite Byzantine mosaics; and, the ruins of Omayyad-dynasty buildings whose existence had been totally unknown.

The ascent from Jericho to Jerusalem (10) is like a pilgrimage to the sky. Upon the flowing hill-tops, the Holy City's spires stretch heavenwards, slender A-Tur on the one hand, sober Augusta Victoria on the other.

Near the Church of St. Peter in Gallicantu on Mt. Zion lies a flight of steps (12) which connected the upper and lower quarters of the city in Roman and Byzantine days. The present-day church, which belongs to the Catholic order of the Assumption, was built over the remains of what is believed to have been the palace of the High Priest Caiaphas. It was here that Peter denied Jesus, as the Master had predicted: "Before the cock crows twice, ye shall deny me thrice." (Mark 14:30.) "And as Peter was beneath the palace, there cometh one of the maids of the High Priest, and when she saw Peter warming himself, she looked upon him and said 'And thou also was with Jesus of Nazareth.' But he denied, saying, 'I know not, neither understand I what thou sayest.' And he went out into the porch and the cock crew ... And a maid saw him again, and he denied it again ... and then again. And a second time, the cock crew. And Peter called to mind the word that Jesus had said ... and he wept." (Mark 14:66—72.)

8. The Roman road from Beth-Phage to Jericho.
9. The road from Mount Zion to the Dung Gate.
10. The modern highway from Jerusalem to Jericho.
11. The Mount of Olives as seen from the Garden of Gethsemane.
12. The Roman-Byzantine steps near the Church of St. Peter in Gallicantu.
13. The modern highway to Jerusalem.

14

And so to the treasure house of Jerusalem: the Old City, secure within the superb Ottoman ramparts built by the Turkish Emperor Suleiman the Magnificent in the 16th century. Skilfully adapted to the contours of the land, the Old City walls have survived intact, their pinkish-golden stones glowing with an almost theatrical splendour.

Suleiman rebuilt the ramparts on the site of Jerusalem's earlier fortifications, vestiges of which have been unearthed at the foot of the western wall between Jaffa Gate and Mount Zion. They confirm that as far back as Maccabean times, Jerusalem's defences ran along the line of the Ottoman walls, Romans, Byzantines, Moslems, Crusaders and Turks all having continued the age-long tradition. In the background rises the spire of the Franciscan monastery of St. Saviour, another striking

15

16

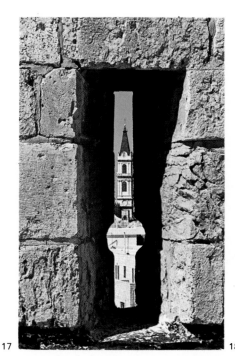

17 18 19

view of which can be seen through a loophole in the ramparts (17), Since 1967, the Old City walls have been cleaned, repaired and restored. The stones employed in the work were brought from the very same quarries said to have been used by Suleiman.

14. Glowing through another slit in the wall is the Dome of the Rock, a jewel in its Ottoman setting.

15. The Ottoman ramparts on Mount Zion, with remains of the ancient wall beneath . . .

16. . . . while at the foot of the eastern ramparts, sheep continue to graze as they have done since time immemorial.

17. The spire of the Franciscan Church of St. Saviour seen from the Phasael Tower.

18. Loopholes in the Ottoman wall near the mosque within the Citadel.

19. A view from the Temple Mount towards the Kidron Valley.

20. David's Citadel mounts guard over the western approaches to the city . . .

21

Damascus Gate is a wonder of pure Moslem architecture. The delicate stone decorations set like a lace edging upon its towers and turrets (21) give to the ensemble an airiness which belies the strength of its construction. The most beautiful of the gates of old Jerusalem, Damascus Gate used to serve as the royal entrance to the city, and so was named in Arabic Bab el Na'asar, the "Triumphal Gateway." The tradition was renewed when the heir to the Prussian throne chose to enter the city through it in 1869. Emperor Franz Joseph of Austria in 1869 and Pope Paul in 1964 did likewise.

The causeway which leads into the gate today (22) was built in 1966/67 to span a British archaeological dig. The excavations revealed part of what might have been an earlier triumphal arch, a Roman one this time, as well as Crusader remains. Nearby, a Roman signpost column stood, hence perhaps another of the gate's Arabic names, Bab el Amud, the Gate of the Pillar. In Hebrew it is known as Sha'ar Shechem, or Nablus Gate, for it is from here that the road to the Samarian capital begins. The Christians, however, preferred the name Damascus Gate because from Nablus the road continues to Damascus, a route of great religious significance in Christian tradition.

St. Stephen's Gate (24) so called by the Christians because St. Stephen is thought to have been stoned to death close by, is called, more descriptively, the Lions' Gate by the Jews. Popular legend has it that two lions (23) appeared in a dream to Suleiman the Magnificent, commanding him to be sure to build a wall around the Holy City for the defence of its citizens. Suleiman dutifully obeyed, and ordered the gate to be embellished with a pair of lions on

22

23

either side of it. Contemporary scholars, however, suspect that the lions may be even older than the Ottoman walls. Because of their similarity to a pair which appear on the Gindas bridge near Ramle, they are thought to have been added to the Jerusalem wall by the same Mameluke king, Bibars, who, in the 13th century, rebuilt the bridge. It is possible that Bibars copied the design from the coat of arms of Prince Edward of England, his sworn enemy.

The only open gate (24) in the ramparts which faces east, the Moslems call its calm shady precincts after Mary who, it is believed, was born not far away. As for the Greeks, they sometimes referred to it as the Gate of Gethsemane.

It was through the Lions' Gate that Israel's soldiers broke into the

21. The beautiful Ottoman decorations on Damascus Gate.
22. The causeway leading into Damascus Gate was built to span the archaeological finds beneath.
23. The lions which flank St. Stephen's Gate.
24. St. Stephen's Gate, also called the Lions' Gate.

25

26

Old City during the Six-Day War in 1967, their courage inspired, perhaps, by its name?

The Golden Gate (27), blocked for nearly a thousand years, stands aloof in an aura of quiet dignity, brooding over the End of Days. The Jews, for whom it is the Gate of Mercy, believe it will be opened only when the Messiah comes; the Moslems conceive it as standing upon the threshold of Heaven and Hell; while to the Christians, it symbolises the fatal entrance of Jesus into the Temple Mount. In memory of this, the gate was opened on Palm Sundays during Crusader times.

The Golden Gate is one of the oldest of Jerusalem's gates to have survived. One of the many Islamic legends woven around it re-

25. The frieze above the Golden Gate, typical of Ottoman architecture.
26. Detail of a Byzantine Corinthian capital inside the Golden Gate.
27. The twin portals of the Golden Gate have been blocked for centuries.
28. Dung Gate near the Western Wall.
29. The triple Hulda Gates in the southern wall of the Temple Mount.
30. "Traffic" of another age through St. Stephen's Gate.

27

lates that the Queen of Sheba presented the monumental entrance pillars as a gift to King Solomon. Suleiman the Magnificent had the Crusader-built wooden gateway replaced with a mighty tower similar to the others which run round the walls. Like them, it is studded with decorative medallions typical of Ottoman architectural design (25). But it is the purity of the late Byzantine archways which confer upon the Golden Gate its air of subdued majesty.

Curiously, Dung Gate (28) has retained its ancient name, acquired no doubt because the city's garbage was deposited not far from the artisans' quarter which lay on the Ophel nearby. The gate was widened during the period of Jordanian rule (1948–1967) to give access to the Jordanian armoured units stationed in the Citadel. But even the modern concrete slab does not detract from the charm of the delicate scalloped arch

which graced the original gateway.

For three millennia, the ascent to the site upon which the Triple Gate (29) stands inspired awe in the hearts of men. From as far back as David's time, the devout made their way from the city on the hill opposite up to the site of the Triple Gate, whence they entered the sacred precincts. Herod carried on the tradition when, a thousand years later, he placed the entrance to his magnificent edifice on the same spot. It was through the Triple Gate — the Hulda Gates of Second Temple days — that pilgrims entered the Temple: even today it is not difficult to imagine Jesus standing at the head of the steps which led up to it, haranguing the crowds as they milled about on holy days and festivals. From the Triple Gate, the faithful passed through a tunnel which ran beneath the mighty outer wall and emerged on the esplanade. The tunnel is still in a perfect state of

28

29

30

31

32

preservation, but, regrettably, is closed to the public. Of Herod's gate, only the doorposts of the eastern gate are still in their original position.

The present gates were built in Crusader times to give the knights direct access to so-called "Solomon's Stables." They were later blocked by the Christians themselves as a defensive measure, and so they have remained to this day.

Set like cameos into the inscrutable old city walls are these delightful medallions bearing sober

floral and geometrical motifs. They are a characteristic feature of Turkish architecture and the frequent use of the Star of David in them has no particular significance (31; 32; 35; 36).

Throughout Jerusalem's history, the Citadel (33; 34) (called "David's Tower" by the Jews), has been one of its most powerful strongholds, for it guards the main entrance to the city from the west. Though its intricate network of steps, loopholes, towers, and ramparts, was intended to render

it impregnable, the structure nevertheless possesses that grace and elegance typical of all the Mameluke and Ottoman architecture of the city. Even its battlements are topped with bell-like decorations similar to those on Damascus Gate, maintaining the artistic unity of the city walls. The turrets which jut out from the towers at the entrance to the citadel, picturesque to the twentieth century eye, in fact played a vital role in the city's defenses. Commanding a bird's eye view of the approaches to the fortress, they compensated for its strategically unfavourable position on low-lying ground.

Since Byzantine days, the Citadel has been associated in popular imagination with the legendary David's Tower evoked in the Song of Songs (4:4): "Thy neck is like the Tower of David, builded with turrets, whereon there hang a thousand shields, all the armour of

33

34

the mighty men." Though evidence for this actually having been the site of the ancient fortress is slim, the name has persisted to this day.

Remains unearthed in recent excavations within the Citadel date from the First Temple, Second Temple, Roman and Byzantine periods. Among them are vestiges of one of the three towers built by Herod to protect his magnificent palace which stood near today's Jaffa Gate. Josephus, meticulous chronicler of the period, left a vivid description of them: "Over against this was the tower Hippicus, and close to it two others, all built by King Herod into the old wall, and for magnitude, beauty and strength without equal in the world. For, apart from his innate magnanimity and his pride in the city, the king sought, in the super-excellence of these works, to gratify his private feelings; dedicating them to the

35

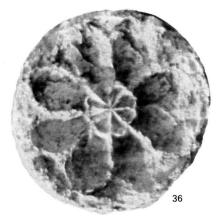

36

memory of three persons to whom he was most fondly attached, and after whom he named these towers — brother, friend and wife." These were Phasael, Hippicus and Mariamne. It is the base of the Phasael tower which can be seen today just inside Jaffa Gate.

During the revolt of the Jews against the Romans, the Citadel was held for a month by the tenacious zealots. They made their last stand there, struggling valiantly against Titus after the rest of the city had fallen.

Josephus tells us further that the Romans took over the fortress after their conquest of the city. "Caesar ordered the whole city and the temple to be razed to the ground, leaving only the loftiest

31/32/35/36. Medallions bearing geometrical motifs embellish the Ottoman walls.
33. The moat around the Citadel (seen from the Phasael Tower).
34. Damascus gate as seen from the inside.
37. A loophole in Damascus Gate.
38. A view over the Citadel courtyard.

37

38

39

40

41

towers, Phasael, Hippicus and Mariamne and the portion of the wall enclosing the city on the west: the latter as an encampment for the garrison that was to remain, and the towers to indicate to posterity the nature of the city and of the strong defences which had yet yielded to Roman prowess." Recently, vestiges of the Tenth Legion — tiles marked with its stamp and traces of the soldiers' living quarters — have been found on the site.

In the Middle Ages, the Citadel was called Pisanum Castellum, for Christian pilgrims associated it with the Hospice of the Knights of Pisa. As for the Moslems, they claim that David was wont to pray on the spot marked by the mosque which they built in the Citadel's precincts in Mameluke times. During Ottoman rule, the Citadel once more served as a military base. Fierce janissaries, their swords drawn mounted guard over it for four hundred years until General Allenby's victorious British forces entered the city and took their place.

The north-eastern tower of the Citadel (38) marks the highest point of the Old City. For Jews everywhere it was for centuries the symbol of Zion, eternal city to which they longed to return. During the tragic years between 1948 and 1967, when Jerusalem was divided, the tower served as an excellent vantage-point for the Jordanian garrison stationed there. From it snipers frequently fired into the heart of Israel's capital which lay spread out like a model at their feet.

Tranquil Zion Gate (41) stands hard by Mount Zion. During the period when it was in Jordanian

hands it remained closed, for it was only a stone's throw from the Israel border which ran along the Mount. Riddled with bullet holes, Zion Gate bears silent testimony to the many unsuccessful attempts which were made by Israel's forces during the War of Independence to fight their way through into the Old City and raise the siege of the nearby Jewish Quarter. A memorial plaque commemorates the breakthrough effected by the Engineer Corps during the Six-Day War.

A Crusader capital (39), decorated with a graceful leaf pattern, protrudes unexpectedly out of the wall near Zion Gate. Many similar ones can be found in Moslem buildings throughout Jerusalem: in most cases they have been reused for decoration. Above the archway, a defensive turret keeps faithful vigil over the approaches to the gate.

Jaffa Gate (43) has always been the main way into Jerusalem. For centuries its flagstones have rung beneath the footsteps of milling multi-coloured crowds converging from everywhere.

In 1898 the entrance proved too narrow to allow Kaiser Wilhelm II's carriage to pass through it, so a breach was made in the wall and moat to permit his official entry into the city. Set beside the original doorway is the 16th-century inscription (42)

39. Hellenistic capital surmounting the Zion Gate.
40. A Crusader capital in second use near Zion Gate.
41. Zion Gate.
42. The Ottoman foundation-stone at Jaffa Gate.
43. Jaffa Gate from the inside: this is the entrance for pedestrians.

42

43

44

45

46

whose elegantly styled arabesques commemorate the pride of Suleiman the Magnificent's reign — the reconstruction of the Old City walls. It is topped by three columns in secondary use.

A few steps from the gateway lie the tombs of the two Ottoman builders who were responsible for the execution of the Sultan's ambitious enterprise. According to legend, Suleiman beheaded them when he discovered that they had not included David's tomb within the Old City walls.

The New Gate into the Christian Quarter of the Old City was breached at the end of the 19th century. Through it, the inhabitants of the Quarter could walk straight out of the city walls, and across to the Notre Dame de France compound opposite. The Notre Dame buildings were constructed about the same time as the gate.

Damascus Gate (44) is the lowest lying of all the city's entrances, and so its defenses had to be reinforced with corner turrets. The loophole on the left of the one shown here was widened in modern times, as were the other loopholes in the walls, so that firearms could by aimed from them.

The south-eastern corner of the Temple Mount (46): a saga in stone towering against Jerusalem's enamel-blue sky. The upper layer dates from the Ottoman period, the middle from Mameluke times, while beneath, the monumental courses of Herod's mighty building works are clearly distinguishable by their smoothly chiselled margins.

This is the meeting point of two of the four walls (45) which Herod had to build in order to shore up the esplanade around his reconstructed Temple. Alongside are remains of what appear to have been the Byzantine city ramparts built in Empress Eudocia's time. Within the walls at the southeast corner are a series of underground chambers leading into "Solomon's Stables." One of them is called the Cradle of Jesus for, according to Christian tradition, it was here that Mary laid her son when she came to pray at the Temple. It is also said that Jesus was tempted by Satan here.

Josephus tells us that, in Second Temple times, a priest used to stand atop the western extremity of the southern wall — the southwest corner of the Temple Mount — and from there blow a trumpet to announce the beginning of the Sabbath and festivals. During the excavations which began here in 1968, a stone was found almost precisely on the spot, on which were engraved in fine Hebrew script the words "To the place of trumpeting . . ." There can be no doubt that it fell from atop the south-western corner during the destruction of the Temple by Titus in 70 A.D. and that it remained there until its rediscovery.

To the left of the picture (45) are vestiges of a 7th–8th century Omayyad temple. It was apparently built with stones which had once been part of the Herodian building complex.

47

44. Detail of the upper façade of Damascus Gate.
45. The south-western corner of the Temple Mount.
46. The south-eastern corner.
47. The façade above Jaffa Gate.
48. A mosque at New Gate in the Christian Quarter
49. El Aqsa mosque shimmers above the southern wall of the Temple Mount

48

49

50

51

52

The Second Temple period covers approximately 600 years, from the return of the Babylonian exiles in the sixth century B.C., to the destruction of Jerusalem by the Romans in 70 A.D. Following the call of Cyrus, King of Persia, to the Jews to return to their homeland, the Temple was rebuilt by the returnees, but it was a small and simple structure compared with the First Temple built by Solomon.

After the conquest of the East by Alexander the Great in 332 B.C., the land changed hands several times between his heirs, the Ptolemaic rulers of Egypt and the Seleucid Empire of Syria. The oppressive regime of the Seleucids culminated in the desecration of the Temple and touched off the Hasmonean revolt. Judah the Maccabee led the rebellion, which ended in the establishment of an independent Jewish state. The Temple became the centre of Jewish life for the Hasmonean Kingdom and Jewish communities elsewhere.

King Herod's ambitious project enlarged the Temple Mount and reconstructed the Temple itself. The vast complex was one of the marvels of the ancient world. The retaining walls around the Mount supported the artificial fill, and subterranean structures, including cisterns and cavernous halls, were so strong that substantial portions have lasted to this day. The most famous section of the outer walls is the Western or "Wailing" Wall (52). The elevated esplanade of the Temple Mount was reached from the south by a wide flight of steps leading to the triple "Hulda Gates." On the western side there was a monu-

mental flight of steps, supported on arches, of which "Robinson's arch" (55) is a remnant. The model (50) shows how the Temple looked from a southeastern angle, with the stairway leading to the royal stoa. A coin struck by Bar Kokhba, leader of the revolt against the Romans in 132 A.D., shows the four pillared façade of the Temple (54).

In recent years the stairs, arches and streets at the foot of the southern and eastern walls of the Temple Mount were unearthed, enabling us to visualise the might and beauty of Jerusalem in that period.

50. *Model reconstructing the southern part of the Temple Mount.*
51. *Inscription "to the place of trumpeting" incised in a fallen stone.*
52. *The western wall of the Temple Mount showing "Robinson's Arch."*
53. *A miniature stone sun-dial found in the excavations near the Temple Mount.*
54. *Bar Kokhba silver coin (second century A.D.) showing the Temple façade.*
55. *Monumental stairway leading up to the Hulda Gates in the southern wall.*

54

55

The Western Wall is the symbolic link between all Jews everywhere, since the beginning of the diaspora. For centuries after the destruction of the Second Temple by Titus in 70 A.D., this wall was believed to be the only remnant of Herod's magnificent edifice, and, access to the holy Temple Mount itself being denied to the Jews by the city's overlords, the Wall came to symbolise it. In time it acquired a sacred character of its own. For almost 2,000 years it stood as a sombre reminder of the Jews' lost freedom, a tragedy so great that its anniversary — on the 9th day of Ab — has been observed each year, since 70 A.D., as a day of mourning in Jewish liturgy. For generations Jews went to weep at the Wall for the fate of their nation, so that it became known as "The Wailing Wall."

Only after the reunification of Jerusalem in 1967, nineteen years after the restoration of the Jewish state, the Wall returned to Jewish hands. The sight of Israel's battle-scarred soldiers, weeping when they reached the hallowed site, remains engraved forever in the memories of those who had the privilege to witness it. Since that historic day, hundreds of thousands of Jews from every corner of

the world have been able to come and go freely and pray at the Wall unhindered. In the past decade, extensive archaeological excavations have revealed much of the Second Temple complex, showing what a magnificent place it was, but the Western Wall has not lost its sanctity.

The history of Jerusalem is witnessed by the stones of the Western Wall. The seven top courses, dating from the end of the Ottoman period, were added in the 19th century by the English-Jewish philanthropist Sir Moses Montefiore, one of modern Jerusalem's foremost famous benefactors. Below them is an intermediate layer constructed earlier. The stones are larger but are not dressed. Below these are the seven Herodian courses, massive rectangular blocks of limestone, with their characteristic, finely-chiselled margins, laid without the use of mortar. Beneath ground level are another 18 or 19 courses resting upon the bedrock.

Contrary to common belief, the Western Wall was not part of the Temple itself, but was one of the four retaining walls which Herod built to support the enlarged esplanade where the Temple stood, or a part of the wall surrounding the outer courtyard. Public buildings and small shops at the foot of

59. Wilson's Arch is named after Sir Charles Wilson, a British archaeologist who was among the founders of the British Palestine Exploration Society established in the second half of the 19th century.

The arch is a remnant of a huge viaduct which linked the Temple Mount with the Upper City in Second Temple times. The dimensions show the magnitude of the Herodian complex of Temple, palace and fortresses. The bridge served not only for pedestrians but also as an aqueduct for the water which was brought from Solomon's Pools to the Temple Mount. The site is now a Jewish place of worship.

57

58

56. Evening prayers at the Western Wall. Pictured is the northern half of the plaza, for men only. The women's section is the southern half. To the left is the passage to "Wilson's Arch."
57. A worshipper praying at the Wall.
58. The notes inserted between the stones of the Western Wall bear the deepest wishes and prayers of the faithful, who believe that they will reach the Holy Presence, which hovers over the site.

the Western Wall catered to the throngs of Jewish pilgrims who came to the Temple on the three great annual festivals. Josephus' "Antiquities of the Jews" describes these edifices and their social uses. The Romans left the supporting walls of the Temple Mount standing to serve as a testimony of the might of the Roman empire.

A visitor to the Western Wall may notice scraps of paper pressed into the cracks between the stones; Orthodox and less observant Jews write on them special requests addressed to the *Shekhinah*, the Divine Presence which, according to popular belief, hovers over the Western Wall.

At the most solemn moment in the Jewish calendar, at sunset on Yom Kippur (the Day of Atonement), when God seals the destiny of each and everyone for the coming year, thousands flock to the Western Wall in a final act of repentance. The dramatic sound of the *shofar* (ram's horn), which marks the end of the day rings out across the square, and the golden stones turn from grey to silver under the moonlight.

60/61/62. The vast rectangular stones with their neatly chiselled margins, seen in these pictures, are characteristic of the Herodian style of construction. Another 18 courses are below ground level.

Devout Jewish men put on the talith *(prayer-shawl) and* tefillin *(phylacteries) every day except on the Sabbath and festivals. But many come to the* Kotel *(the Wall) to make a special prayer on a happy occasion, such as the Bar Mitzvah ceremony, when a boy reaches his religious majority at the age of thirteen.*

The huge dimensions of the Wall notwithstanding, there appears to be something close and intimate in the devotions of these men reading the ancient prayers before it.

61

63

Jerusalem is full of holy sites around which legends have been woven over the centuries. Sometimes they mark events, sometimes they perpetuate the memory of venerable sages. One of these is the burial cave of Simon the Just (66). According to tradition, Simon lived in the fourth century B.C. In 332 B.C., when Alexander the Great invaded the Land of Israel, he is said to have come out, together with the sages of Jerusalem, to welcome the conqueror. Josephus tells us that the meeting took place on Mt. Scopus (*Antiquities* 11:8, 5). The cave where Simon is believed to be buried is hewn out of the rock and contains niches where the coffins of his disciples are believed to have been placed. He himself is supposed to have been laid to rest in an adjoining chamber. In the past, when natural disasters struck the city, Jews used to come and pray at Simon's tomb. Today the festival of Lag Ba-omer is celebrated here.

The Tiferet Israel Synagogue (64) was one of the most magnificent in the Old City of Jerusalem. Its dome was one of the highest within the walls, and from it a splendid view of Jerusalem could be seen. The synagogue, built towards the end of the 1860's, was better known as the synagogue of Nissan Bek, for it was he who inspired its construction and was responsible for its management until 1890.

Curiously, it was the Austrian Emperor Franz Joseph who helped put the final touch to the building. When he visited the city in 1869, the dome was still unfinished, and thanks to his generous donation it could be completed.

Because of its elevated location, the Tiferet Israel Synagogue

64

65

served as a lookout post for the beleaguered Jews of the Old City during the War of Independence. The Jordanians tried to take it, and in the fighting the building was totally destroyed. Its reconstruction has not yet begun.

The Yohanan ben Zakkai Synagogue (65) belongs to the Sephardi community, and is thought to stand on the site where Rabban (Great Rabbi) Yohanan Ben Zakkai used to teach, before the destruction of the Second Temple. There is a legend that a tunnel connects the synagogue with the Temple Mount. The Ben Zakkai complex, made up of several interconnecting structures, was built over a period of four hundred years, each building added as the need arose. The Eliyahu Hanavi (Elijah the Prophet) Synagogue is the oldest of these, and was probably built in the 16th century. During the War of Independence, the synagogue buildings served as a shelter for the Jewish inhabitants of the Old City who were besieged in their Quarter. Since 1967, they have been restored to their former beauty.

"And Rachel died and was buried in the way to Ephrath, which is Bethlehem" (Gen.

66

35:19). According to an ancient tradition, the reason Jacob buried his wife here was because the Ingathering of Exiles would pass along this way, and Rachel would intercede for mercy on their behalf.

Until the 18th century the tomb consisted of twelve stones laid, according to tradition, by Jacob and his eleven sons. It acquired its present form in stages as, over the years, parts were added on to it. Moses Montefiore found the tomb in a state of utter ruin when he visited it at the end of the 19th century, and it was he who saw to its restoration. When the great philanthropist died, earth from Rachel's tomb was scattered around his grave in London.

63. The Holy Ark recently brought from Italy to grace the Eliyahu Hanavi Synagogue is one of the most superb examples of Sephardi artistry which have come down to us.
64. The main entrance to the Tiferet Israel Synagogue.
65. One of the twin Holy Arks of the Yohanan ben Zakkai synagogue.
66. The grave of Simon the Just is draped with richly embroidered coverings.
67. The draping on Rachel's tomb is embroidered with the verse 31:15 from Jeremiah.

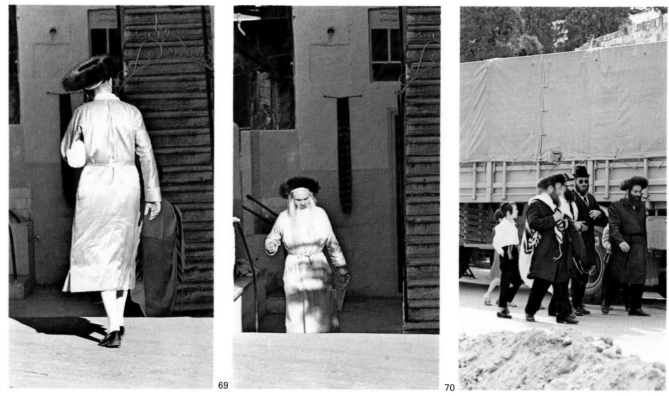

68 69 70

The fascinating quarter of Mea Shearim inhabited by Orthodox Jews and the communal life within it revolves around the many synagogues and the *yeshivot* (religious seminaries) where, from morning to night, devout Jews indulge in the study of the Torah and its commentaries. Like most religious communities, the Jews of Mea Shearim are highly conservative in their way of life.

They dress in the style of their forefathers in the ghettoes of Eastern Europe, and they make no concessions to the temptations of modern society. They conduct life according to the letter of the Jewish Law, as promulgated through the centuries, and its study and fulfilment are their real joy. They seldom have recourse to Israel's secular law-courts, preferring to resolve their differences according to religious injunction.

Zedakah, charity, is scrupulously practiced: within the quarter are a hostel and a soup-kitchen for the needy, and special funds for indigent brides. Many of the breadwinners of Mea Shearim earn their living from small businesses, working only enough to provide their family with a modest income, while their spare time is devoted to religious study. A common sight in the narrow streets of the quarter

71

72

73

74

is a man carrying a "sandwich board" to call the faithful to prayer and to announce momentous news.

Built in the 1870's, Mea Shearim was one of the first quarters to be built outside the Old City walls. Because of its isolation, the inhabitants had to protect themselves from the marauders who plagued Jerusalem at that time. They built their houses cheek by jowl, so that the unbroken outer walls would form a kind of protective rampart. The courtyard entrances were fitted with iron gates that were closed at night, and wells were dug within to ensure an independent water supply. The name Mea Shearim, literally "a hundred gates" or "a hundredfold," was probably derived from Genesis 26:12 — "And Isaac sowed in that land, and found in the same year a hundredfold," a verse symbolic of success and plenty.

Visitors to Mea Shearim, particularly women, are advised to dress modestly so as not to incur the wrath of the pious with a display of low necklines or bare legs. Placards in Hebrew, English and Yiddish (73) warn the unsuspecting in advance, requesting them to comport themselves with due decency within the quarter.

On holy festivals the Orthodox Jew wears a white robe like a shroud, to remind him of his final destination, and on his head the fur hat, originally worn by his forebears in Poland at the command of a Saxon king, who sought to make them ridiculous in the eyes of their wives — and in the end it became an honoured headgear. The *talith*, fringed prayer shawl, is worn over the shoulders, as ordained by the Law from Mount Sinai.

68/69. The inhabitants of Mea Shearim in their traditional dress entering the synagogue.
70. Orthodox men wearing the characteristic streimel, *fur hat, and the ritual prayer shawl.*
71. The largest Yeshiva, or religious academy, in Mea Shearim, where the pious study day and night.
72. Charity begins at home.
73. One of the hoardings in the quarter requesting "Daughters of Israel to dress modestly."
74. A greengrocer in Mea Shearim.

75

76

77

The city of Jerusalem at the time of the Second Temple had its burial grounds outside the walls and some of the tombs which dotted the slopes can be seen to this day. Most of them were hewn out of the bedrock; some are plain graves, others are monuments embellished with decorated façades. Modest graves were in a simple burial chamber, whose walls were honeycombed with a number of loculi. The wealthier citizens built more elaborate monuments to perpetuate their memory.

Though each tomb has its own special character, all are of eastern Hellenistic architectural style: Doric and Ionic motifs are frequently found on the capitals of the columns and in the frieze decorations, but no trace of the Corinthian style has been found in any of these tombs. Egyptian influence shows in the pyramidlike structures, and in the use of the concave cornice.

In the Kidron Valley, opposite the Temple Mount, lie the four most famous tombs of Jerusalem, all of them rock-hewn. They are known respectively as the Tomb of Zecharia (75), the Tomb of Bnei Hezir (78) (also called the Grotto of St. James), the Pillar of Absalom (80), and the Tomb of Jehoshaphat (76). Except for Bnei Hezir, these names have no basis in historical fact. They simply grew out of the legends which were woven around the monuments over the centuries.

The tomb which is sometimes called the Grotto of St. James (78) belonged, in fact, to the priestly Hezir family of the First Temple period. The Hebrew inscription engraved on the monu-

ment, one of the oldest ever discovered, states that members of this family were buried inside. This monument is the earliest Jewish construction in Doric style to be discovered in Jerusalem.

The name "Grotto of St. James" comes from the Christian belief that Jacob ben Halfi — the Apostle St. James — was buried here. Jewish legend relates that Azariah, King of Judah, dwelt here after he was struck with leprosy and was forbidden to enter the city. (II Kings, 15:5.) Because the king then was freed of all his obligations, the site was also called *Beit ha-Hofshit*, the free, or separate, house.

The Tomb of Zechariah (77 to the right), a pyramid-like structure which stands to the right of

75. *A view of the Hezir tomb and the Tomb of Zechariah.*
76. *The frieze of Jehoshaphat's tomb.*
77. *A view of the Kidron Valley: the slopes at the foot of the south-east corner of the Temple Mount are in the foreground, the Mount of Olives on the horizon.*
78. *The Hezir family tomb.*
79. *Tombstones on the Mount of Olives, the Jews' ancient and most sacred cemetery.*
80. *The Pillar of Absalom.*

79

80

81

the Hezir monument, is carved entirely out of the rock, and is surrounded by high walls. Along its four sides run columns with ornamental capitals. Though the building is of the Second Temple period, it cannot be precisely dated.

For centuries the Jews have buried their dead near Zechariah's tomb, for the monument bestowed on the surroundings an aura of sanctity. As its name implies, it was believed to be the grave of the prophet Zechariah, who chastised the Children of Israel for breaking the Lord's commandments, and foresaw the destruction of the Temple. It is said that the high priests had a hand in the murder of Zechariah, when he came to the Temple on the Day of Atonement. The deep guilt which weighed on the conscience of the Jews only added to the holiness of the monument, so that in time the faithful became accustomed to praying there. They would implore for mercy when times were hard, for rain when drought struck the region. Once in the days of Mohammed Ali, when winter came, when the rains did not fall and famine threatened the land, the governor summoned the Jews and threatened them with a dire fate if rain did not fall within the week. The hapless Jews went to the Tomb of Zechariah and prayed continuously for three whole days. Towards evening on the last day, the skies clouded over, the first drops fell, and they were saved.

The Pillar of Absalom (80) is one of the most impressive of the tombs of Jerusalem, as much for its architectural form as for its

82

81. The façade of the Tomb of the Kings.
82. The entrance to the Tomb of the Kings. To the left is the stone which sealed the opening.
83. The façade of Jason's Tomb.
84. One of the tombs of the Sanhedria complex with its ornamental façade.

with acanthus leaves, vines and fruit motifs, all of them typical of Jewish art in Second Temple times. As the name implies, it was believed to be the tomb of King Jehoshaphat.

The Tomb of the Kings (81), a regal monument indeed, lies north of Damascus Gate. It is believed to have been the last resting place of the proselyte Queen Helena of Adiabene, who was buried in Jerusalem in 50 A.D. As Josephus noted, the façade of the tomb is richly ornamented: with the grape and acanthus designs typical of the Judaeo-Hellenistic period. According to popular Jewish tradition, the Tomb of the Kings was the burial place of Kalba Savua, a pious —

and wealthy — Jew of the Second Temple period, who was the father in-law of Rabbi Akiva.

Jason's Tomb (83) is in western Jerusalem, in the heart of the Rehavia residential district. No one knows who this Jason was, to whom the Aramaic inscription on the tomb refers, and it is thought that he may have been a high priest in the Second Temple.

The Tomb of Saṇhedria (84) shows examples of Jewish Art in the Second Temple period. The tombs were decorated on the outside with very beautiful floral ornamentation. The interior of the tombs was hewn out of limestone rock in the form of loculi, in which were interred the remains of the dead.

excellent state of preservation. Standing by itself beside the valley, its conical roof gives it a quaint, almost exotic charm. The base of the monument is square and its four sides are embellished with columns. The upper portion, built of hewn stones, is circular, and on it stands the cone.

The popular belief that this is the tomb of Absalom had had curious consequences: because Absalom, son of King David, rebelled against his father, devout Jews, Christians and Moslems would throw stones at this monument whenever they went past it, with the result that in time it was covered with stones!

The Tomb of Jehoshaphat (76), not far from Absalom's Pillar, was probably built at the same time as its neighbour and planned along similar lines. It has an impressive entrance whose decorative tympanum is engraved

The lyrical tale of Naomi and Ruth, gleaning in the wheat fields of Bethlehem, has left an indelible mark on the minds of countless generations brought up in the Judeo-Christian tradition. From Ruth descended David, the stripling who used to play like an angel upon his harp as he tended his father's flocks in the nearby pastures. According to Christian belief Jesus, direct descendant of David, was like him born in Bethlehem, and so in time the town became sacred to all Christendom. The account of the birth of Jesus, as told by the Apostles, is in keeping with an ancient tradition which attributed exceptional characteristics to the birth of other biblical characters, among them Isaac, Samson and Samuel.

The story of the Church of the Nativity is less turbulent than that of the Holy Sepulchre. In 135 A.D. after the last Jewish rebellion led by Bar Kokhba had been suppressed, Hadrian built a pagan temple on the site, and it was not until 324 A.D. when Constantine proclaimed Christianity the official religion of the Holy Roman Empire, that it was rediscovered. Constantine's mother Helena, a zealous convert to the new religion, encouraged her son to commemorate Jesus' birthplace with a basilica that was to be embellished with fine mosaic floors, marble

wall panels and intricate decorations. However, this splendid edifice lasted only about three hundred years. In the 6th century, during Justinian's time, it was destroyed, and another built in its place. Fortunately, the new church escaped the ravages wrought on Christian property by the Persians during their conquest of the Holy Land in the following century. Legend tells that the mosaic on the western façade of the church depicted among other personages, rulers of the Persian Empire. The conquerors were apparently so impressed by this that they left the building untouched.

Rather unexpectedly, the early Arabian Omayyad dynasty (7th century) dealt kindly with Bethlehem; a small locality, it would have had little chance of protecting itself against the Arabian invaders. However, after its conquest, Caliph

88

85. The roof of the Church of the Nativity dates only from 1842. After the Ottoman Turks had removed the **leaden one to melt the metal down** *for ammunition, wooden beams had to be brought from Constantinople to replace it.*

It took three months for the caravan of oxen to make its way from the port of Jaffa to Bethlehem, and the road had to be specially widened to let it pass.
86. The entrance to the fortress-like Church of the Nativity is hard to discern. It is low and narrow and there is just enough room for one person at a time to pass through it.

This is, of course, not the original doorway: the 6th-century portal which can be seen in the wall above the opening was blocked to prevent the Mamelukes from entering the church on horseback.
87. Down the main body of the church runs a double row of pillars which have **survived from the 6th-century edifice.** *Of typical late Byzantine style, they are made of local stone which pilgrims often mistake for marble.*

During the Crusader period, the pillars were embellished with the portraits of saints, remains of which attest to their fine artistry.
88. The Iconastasis which divides the apse from the main body of the church.

The chased silver portraits of Mary and Jesus which decorate it were donated by the Russian Orthodox Church in the 19th century.
89. The pulpit
90. The tapers of the faithful.

89   90

91

92

Omar visited the town and guaranteed the Christians freedom of worship. Indeed, he even prayed there. Once again, the church was saved.

On the whole, relations between Christianity and Islam were cordial in Bethlehem, so that the Church of the Nativity was spared the wholesale destruction of Jerusalem's churches, ordered by the fanatical el-Hakim. Nevertheless, the number of Christian inhabitants of Bethlehem fell sharply during the period of Moslem rule.

Like the Church of the Holy Sepulchre, the Church of the Nativity was one of the most important holy places which the Crusaders set out to conquer. As a symbol of their victory, Baldwin I held his coronation ceremony there on Christmas Day, 1100: the first Crusader king to be crowned.

Ten years later, the church was raised by the Pope to the status of cathedral and the first Bishop of Bethlehem was consecrated. A large-scale restoration of the building was undertaken shortly afterwards, and Bethlehem itself thrived as pilgrims flocked to it.

Moslem rule returned with the defeat of the Crusaders at the Battle of the Horns of Hittin in 1187. At first the Church of the Nativity was unaffected and life in Bethlehem went on as before, but as time went by, the Christians began to lose their control over the holy places.

The era of religious tolerance ended abruptly with the advent of the Mameluke ruler Bibars. Christians were expelled from Bethlehem and pilgrims were prohibited to set foot in it. Inevitably, the Church of the Nativity fell on sad days. The few Christians who had remained in the town were forbidden to repair the building, and its architectural unity was seriously damaged as a result. On more than one occasion Moslems pillaged the church, carrying off decorations for their own constructions.

93

94

91. The star which marks the spot where Jesus was born. Each of its fourteen points symbolises one of the Stations of the Cross.
An inscription above reads: "Hic de Virgine Maria Jesus Christus natus est" — "Here Jesus Christ was born to the Virgin Mary."
92. The space under the Church of the Nativity where St. Jerome was buried, after having lived there for many years during his work at the Monastery. A famous tradition tells of wild beasts who came and joined the saint in his cell, lying meekly at his feet.
93. Paula, Eustochium and St. Jerome were buried in the same crypt.
94. A detail above an iron door located inside the Greek Orthodox Monastery of the Church of the Nativity.
95. It was in this cell that the Dalmatian monk, St. Jerome, is believed to have translated the Bible into the Latin.
  He was among the many monks who in the 4th century came to live in and around the holy places. St. Jerome was accompanied to Bethlehem by two Roman ladies of noble birth, Paula and her daughter Eustochium. Both a convent and a monastery, later to become known as the House of St. Jerome, were built at Paula's behest. Though the location of these two buildings has not been determined, it would seem that the monastery in which St. Jerome lived and worked was attached to the Church of the Nativity and stood on the site now occupied by the Franciscan monastery.

95

96

97

98

The authorities did little to prevent them — the guard they mounted over the Christian holy places was purely symbolic.

In Ottoman days friction developed between the various sects over the possession of the church, the core of the dispute being between the Greek Orthodox Church and the Catholic Franciscan order. The affair became so enmeshed in politics that the mysterious disappearance of the silver star which had marked Jesus' birthplace served as one of the immediate pretexts for the Crimean war.

After this war, which ended in 1858, the Turkish Sultan granted a *firman* which also contained a guarantee of the status quo in the various Holy Sanctuaries. But, despite this *firman* and other religious privileges which were granted at that time disputes still occurred between the different Christian sects.

The 19th century saw the revival of pilgrim traffic to Bethlehem, and with it the town prospered once again. In recent years the Church of the Nativity has been under constant repair. Every Christmas Eve, celebrations reach their climax when, at midnight, the colourful Franciscan procession leaves the adjoining Catholic church to enter the Crypt.

Every year on Christmas Eve, the bells of rejoicing peal out from Bethlehem. The ones shown here are in the belfry of the Greek Orthodox Monastery, which commands a breathtaking view of the biblical landscape of the Judaean hills just south of Jerusalem. The Armenian monastery has its steeple too, towering above the atrium of the Church of the Nativity on whose southern wall it stands.

96. Detail of a door in the Greek Orthodox Monastery of the Nativity.
97. This carved stone, depicting St. George killing the Dragon, is in the courtyard which separates the church from the Greek Orthodox Monastery.
98. The Franciscan church adjoining the Church of the Nativity was built in 1882 to replace a mediaeval one which was thought to have stood on the remains of the Monastery of St. Jerome.
99. A bird's-eye view of the roof of the Church of the Nativity.
100. The roof of the Church of the Nativity. From this angle, the transepts and apse of the original building of Justinian can be clearly seen.

99

The Armenian monastery (102) stands on the south side of the courtyard of the Church of the Nativity. Architectural and archaeological remains have been uncovered within its walls, probably belonging to the Byzantine and Crusader periods. The early history of the Armenian community in Bethlehem is uncertain, but Armenian documents from the 7th and 8th centuries attest to the presence of Armenian communities in the city during Justinian's rule. The Armenians seem to have left Bethlehem in the 7th century owing to dissension within their leadership. Some scholars believe that parts of the monastery were built in the 17th century by the Armenian patriarch Krikor Baronder.

The atmosphere of the Armenian monastery is typical of the ancient churches of the east, and the site is well worth a visit. The mediaeval hall, known as the School of St. Jerome, was probably built in the 12th century. It is decorated with two parallel rows of vaults, and a line of pillars runs down the centre. The pilgrim Quaresmius relates that the hall was either St. Jerome's library or the place where he taught. This appears unlikely, however, for the School of St. Jerome stands on the courtyard of Justinian's time and probably belongs to a later period. The building was used as a stable in Quaresmius' times.

101/103/104. A view of the Church bells which are located inside the Greek Orthodox Monastery.
102. The Armenian Church steeple in the foreground and the Greek Orthodox Church steeple in the background.
105. A general view of Bethlehem.

101

102

103

104

105

THE CHURCHES OF BETHLEHEM

The Syrian Orthodox community of Bethlehem numbers some 2,000 souls, and its life revolves around its modern church and primary school. Work began on St. Mary's Church in 1928 and was completed in the 'thirties. Beneath it are remains of what is thought by the Syrians to be of the Byzantine church which was destroyed during the Moslem conquest, rebuilt by the Crusaders and destroyed once again by the Mamelukes. The ancient church is called after St. Ephraim, who lived from 303 to 373 A.D., before the great schism in the Christian Church. St. Ephraim, writer and poet, lived in southern Turkey and, according to the Syrian sect of Palestine, was the author both of the liturgy of the Syrian Church and a commentary on the New Testament. He is an acknowledged saint of most Christian churches and sects.

106. The cupola of the Syrian Orthodox Church, in the foreground, while on the horizon can be seen the minaret of an Islamic mosque.
107. The German Lutheran Christian Church of Bethlehem which was consecrated in the 1890's.
108. A Greek Orthodox monk in the Church of the Nativity.
109. A general view of the Antonio Belloni Church.
110. A view of Bethlehem with the Mosque and the churches.
111. This Catholic Church serves the Bethlehem University today.

106

107

108

109

110

111

112

113

The Cenacle, or Upper Room on Mt. Zion (114), is believed to be the place where Jesus, with his disciples, partook of the Last Supper before he was seized by the Romans in Gethsemane. The room is also associated with the events related in the Acts of the Apostles 2:1—4, according to which on the feast of Pentecost, fifty days after Passover, the Holy Spirit descended upon the disciples in a blaze of fire. The building is typical of 12th-century Crusader architecture, as the capital of the pillar and the Gothic arches of the interior demonstrate. In the background is the *mihrab* (prayer niche) built by the Moslems in the wall facing Mecca, in 1928.

The original Cenacle was part of a private dwelling of Second Temple times, and probably stood not far from the present edifice. After the Crusader conquest in 1099, the Christian knights built, in the traditional place of this shrine, the Church of St. Mary of Zion with the present Cenacle in its southern wing.

112. A 16th century votive inscription inside the Hall of the Cenacle which mentions the name of Sultan Suleiman.
113. A Corinthian capital supporting one of the arches.
114. The Cenacle (Room of the Last Supper).

114

The Via Dolorosa is among the holiest sites in Christendom. It is the path taken by Jesus when he left the Praetorium after his trial and, bearing his cross on his back, made his way to the place of crucifixion on Golgotha. It was the custom in Roman times to oblige those who had been condemned to death to walk through the main streets of the city with their name and details about their conviction clearly displayed, so that they might "see and be seen."

At first sight, the Via Dolorosa seems no different from any other street in the Old City, except perhaps for its picturesque archways, with their interplay of light and shade a closer look reveals the churches erected at the nine stations of the cross which lie along it. (The remaining five are within the Church of the Holy Sepulchre.) The shrines bear the number of the stations they represent, each one commemorating one of the dramatic incidents which occurred on Jesus' last journey.

It was only in the 14th century that the Via Dolorosa acquired its spiritual significance. At that time, the western world was going through a profound spiritual crisis caused by constant religious strife, and the interminable Hundred Years' War between England and France. The tribulations of the people took on religious overtones and were likened to the suffering of Jesus on the Via Dolorosa, a symbol which found frequent expression in mediaeval art and literature. It was at this time that the Franciscan friars held their first Friday afternoon procession along

115. A general view of the Via Dolorosa.

the Via Dolorosa, carrying heavy crosses on their backs in memory of the suffering of their Master. The custom has survived to this day, and many pilgrims join the weekly ceremony.

The exact route of the Via Dolorosa is still disputed by scholars, as are the sites of the stations along it. Only some of these are mentioned in the New Testament, others having their roots in popular tradition. In the 16th century the location of the Praetorium was determined as having been within the Antonia fortress. One of the reasons for this was that the Moslem Mayor of Jerusalem had chosen the fortress as his residence, and had installed

the local law court within it. The association was clear. However, the first station was fixed north of the Praetorium because entry to the fortress was forbidden to the Christians under Moslem rule. The rest of the Way of the Cross was given its present form only in the 19th century.

In mediaeval times, it was customary in European churches to reconstruct the Via Dolorosa, so that those of the pious who could not reach Jerusalem could do so in their own lands.

The Lithostratos, a Greek word meaning pavement, lies beneath the Convent of the Sisters of Zion and the Monastery of the Flagellation. It is composed of huge pav-

ing stones believed to have been part of the courtyard of the Antonia fortress where Jesus was tried. Grooves were chiselled into the blocks to prevent horses from slipping on their smooth surface. Some of them are engraved with the designs of games such as knuckle-bones and the Game of the King, with which the Roman guards are believed to have amused themselves during the trial. The stones of the Lithostratos cover two huge water reservoirs which

116. This inscription was found in the Convent of St. Etienne during an archaeological dig conducted by members of the Dominican Order in the 19th century. It is dedicated to the Emperor Hadrian.

117. In 1889, when the Casa Nova in Bethlehem was in the process of construction, thirteen bells, apparently dating from the 13th or 14th century, were uncovered. Once part of the Church of the Nativity, they were transferred for safekeeping to the Museum of the Flagellation.

118. This magnificent prayer book is on display in the Museum of the Flagellation.

119. A close-up of the Game of the King, one of the many amusements which were part of the Roman Saturnalia festivities. The soldiers would choose a dummy king, address it by all the titles worthy of such rank, and give it full liberty to indulge its desires and instincts. They then would torture and kill it.

120. The Lithostratos pavement located at the Ecce Homo.

121. A part of the three-entrance triumphal arch built by Hadrian at the Ecce Homo.

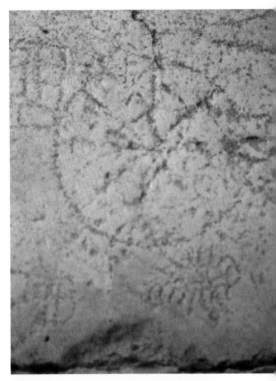

119

120

121

supplied the fortress in the Second Temple times. Frequently mentioned in Greek documents, the reservoir is known by the name Struthion. This is apparently a Greek derivative of the word for Bunting, a bird common in the Holy Land.

On the western limit of the Lithostratos stands a triple triumphal arch known as the Ecce Homo. Tradition tells us that through this arch Jesus passed into the Via Dolorosa after his trial. Scholars consider that both the **Lithostratos** and the **Ecce Homo** arch were built by Hadrian after the suppression of the Bar Kokhba revolt in 135 A.D. as part of a small Roman forum. The Antonia fortress probably lay south-east of the site.

The northern arch of the Ecce Homo (121) can be seen in the Convent of the Sisters of Zion, where it serves as a background to the altar. Only the upper portion of the archway can be seen, for the lower part is concealed beneath the present-day floor.

The first and second stations of the cross are located nearby. The first commemorates verse 28 in Chapter 18 of the Gospel according to St. John: "Then they led Jesus from Caiaphas unto the hall of judgement." The hall of judgement is believed to have been opposite the Convent of the Flagellation where the Omariyya school stands now. The second station is marked by the Convent of the Flagellation and the Convent of the Sisters of Zion. Here Jesus is said to have been whipped, judged, crowned with thorns and led out to the Via Dolorosa.

The Catholic Polish Church commemorates the third station

122

123

124

of the cross (123). The entrance originally led to the Hammam El Sultan—Turkish baths which functioned until 1947. The following year the chapel was rebuilt out of the funds contributed by Polish soldiers who served in the Holy Land during the Second World War. The pillar fragment, now incorporated within the railing, served for years to mark the place where Jesus fell the first time.

The fourth station (125) is believed to be the meeting place between Mary and Jesus. It belongs to the Armenian Catholics who built their shrine in 1881. In the crypt, which lies at the ancient street level, is a huge mosaic floor which came to light while building was in progress. Its wide decorative border surrounds a pair of footprints facing north-west, traditionally believed to be Mary's. The mosaic dates from the 4th to 6th century, Byzantine period, and may have belonged to the St. Sophia Church which once stood here.

122. Detail of the third station.
123. The third station.
124. Detail of the fourth station.
125. The fourth station.

125

126

127

128

129

As Jesus moved along his way, Saint Veronica wiped his face with a damp handkerchief on which the imprint of his features miraculously remained. This is the Sixth Station. The handkerchief is believed to have been brought to the Church of St. Peter's in Rome in 707.

The seventh station (128) commemorates the site where Jesus fell the second time. It is believed to mark the place of the Gate of Judgement which led out of Jerusalem in Second Temple times. The seventh station was purchased by the Franciscans in 1875. Within it is a pillar which was part of the colonnaded Cardo Maximus, the main north-south road which ran through the city in Roman and Byzantine times.

A stone engraved with a Latin cross and a Greek word *Nika* indicates the eighth station (130). The inscription means "Jesus the Christian is victorious." Like the seventh, this station too is believed to have been located outside the city walls of the Second Temple period.

At the entrance to the Coptic Church (131) which adjoins the roof of the Chapel of St. Helena, stands a pillar, the ninth and last station of the cross outside the Holy Sepulchre. It was here that Jesus fell for the third time before reaching the site of his crucifixion.

126. The traditional procession of Christian pilgrims along the Via Dolorosa on Friday afternoons.
127. The sixth station.
128. The seventh station.
129. The fifth station is named after the **pilgrim Simon of Cyrene (Libya) who** *according to the Gospel helped Jesus carry the cross (Luke 23:26).*
130. The eighth station.
131. The ninth station.

130

131

132

A stroller through the lanes and alleys of the Old City comes upon the Church of the Holy Sepulchre almost by accident. Set in the very heart of the Christian Quarter, its massive domes brooding over the rooftops packed around it, it stands as a silent monument to the knights of Mediaeval Christendom, who enthusiastically took up arms, undertook a voyage fraught with danger across a goodly portion of the then-known world, and sacrificed their lives to deliver the hallowed site from the hands of the Infidel. It seems almost miraculous that since the Church's cornerstone was laid by the Crusaders in 1149, it has resisted the series of catastrophes, both natural and man-made, which have struck Jerusalem. There have been fires and earthquakes and conquest after bloody conquest, yet somehow the edifice has survived them all.

From the parvis, the rectangular form of the Holy Sepulchre's sober yet powerful façade can be clearly seen, a heavy cornice dividing the two storeys of the building. The entrance (133) is composed of twin arched portals, one of which has been blocked since Saladin's time. It seems likely that the Crusaders drew their inspiration for the design of the doorway from the Byzantine Golden Gate which to them symbolised the dramatic entrance of Jesus into Jerusalem.

Groups of three green marble pillars standing on high bases flank each doorway. Their capitals are decorated with a pattern of acan-

thus foliage in 6th-century style of Justinian and the juncture between the central pillars is executed with perfect symmetry. Above the doorways the gables are surrounded by a double frieze, the inner one in Goudron style, the outer one in rosette form leading off from the central acanthus medallion. Here too the decoration is reminiscent of the Golden Gate. The rich mosaics which embellished the tympana have unfortunately not come down to us. However, descriptions from Crusader times mention one of them as having depicted the Madonna and Child.

Curiously, though the tympana did not survive, the lintels remained in their original place until the 1930's. After the fire which ravaged the building they were removed for preservation to the Rockefeller Museum. The lintels were conceived as a pair: the one depicts scenes from the life of Jesus, the other is a vision of Hell. The moral is clear to all those entering the sacred spot where Jesus died and was resurrected: better to tread in the footsteps of the Master than to commit one's soul to eternal damnation.

The Church of the Holy Sepulchre stands on a rise called Golgotha, an Aramaic word meaning skull. Christian tradition has it

132. Capitals of columns in the lower section of the façade of the Holy Sepulchre. "Blown in the wind" acanthus leaves are bent into two horizontal bands circling the capital. Above them, classic spirals are draped by an outer covering of the same leaves — a typical Justinian-period design.
133. The entrance to the Church of the Holy Sepulchre.
134. Detail of a Crusader door-post engraved with Christian Crusader symbols.
135. Detail of one of the pillars at the entrance to the Church of the Holy Sepulchre. The crosses were probably engraved by pilgrims.

that the place was so called because the skull of the first human being was found there. Golgotha is commonly believed to have lain outside the city walls of Second Temple times; otherwise it could not have served as a site for executions.

A Roman altar to Aphrodite stood on Golgotha until the fourth century, when Helena, mother of the Byzantine Emperor Constantine, made her famous pilgrimage to Jerusalem and discovered on the rise the grave of Jesus, together with the remains of a number of crosses. In 333 A.D. Constantine ordered a huge basilica to be built on the spot. It was called Anastasis, the Greek word for resurrection, as a reminder that it was here that Jesus rose from the dead. The basilica can be clearly discerned on the Madaba map, a Byzantine pictorial mosaic of Jerusalem from the 6th century.

In 614, the Persians overran the Holy Land, sowing terror and destruction in their wake. Every monastery, church or shrine holy to Byzantium was destroyed. Christians were massacred, and the Church of the Holy Sepulchre put to the torch. The great cross of Golgotha was carried off as booty, and many Christians were led away into captivity.

Fourteen years later the Byzantine Emperor Heraclius overcame the Persians. He made a triumphal entry into Jerusalem through the Golden Gate, carrying before him what was believed to be the cross of Golgotha that had been rescued from enemy hands. The reconstruction of the church was undertaken by Modestus, an Abbot of the Church of the Holy Sepulchre, later appointed Patriarch of Jerusalem.

Jerusalem fell under Arab domination in 638, but the Omayyad conquerors showed greater

tolerance towards the Christians than their predecessors, guaranteeing them freedom of worship and the inviolability of life and property. Legend has it that Scuphronius, Bishop of Jerusalem, invited the Caliph Omar to pray in the basilica. The Arab ruler wisely refused in order to prevent devout Moslems from using his gesture as a pretext to claim the site.

But this period of peaceful co-existence was not to last. In 1009 Caliph el-Hakim ordered the total destruction of the Church of the Resurrection "and all trappings of Christian splendour." His instructions were carried out to the letter. The interior of the church was ransacked and pillaged, the tombstones overturned, and an attempt was even made to uproot the Holy

Grave in order to "wipe out every last trace of it from the face of the earth." So tells Yahia ibn Saud, an 11th-century chronicler.

In 1030 the Cairo Caliphate, at the time master of Jerusalem, authorised the Byzantines to undertake the restoration of the Church, a task which was completed in 1048. However, this did nothing to placate the Franks,

136. The upper part of the Golgotha chapel, also known as the Franks' Room.

137. Another view of the cornice on the Golgotha Chapel.

138/139. Details of a wooden door inside the Church.

137

138

139

whose anger at Hakim's wanton vandalism was still smouldering. Towards the end of the century the Crusaders set out to deliver the Holy Places from Moslem rule. In 1099 they took Jerusalem by storm, and Godfrey of Bouillon was proclaimed Defender of the Holy Sepulchre. Work began at once on the restoration of the Byzantine rotunda under which the Sepulchre itself still stands, and on the construction of the magnificent new cathedral. The Crusaders gave the church its name of the Holy Sepulchre.

Although the twelfth-century structure has remained standing for over eight centuries, it has not been spared the ravages of time. Over the years, spontaneous action was taken by Christians the world over to reinforce it, for it had been weakened by earthquakes, fires, and deliberate acts of destruction. However, their efforts were not coordinated, and as a result the building lost much of its architectural harmony. Large-scale restoration was made the more difficult because of the division of responsibility for the Church among the many different sects who share the edifice. Even after the severe earthquake of 1927 they could not agree on the

140

141

142

143

144

145

measures to be taken, and the only solution was to prop the building up with a metal scaffolding to prevent its total collapse.

The rights and possessions of each sect represented in the Holy Sepulchre — Greek Orthodox, Roman Catholic, Armenian, Coptic, Ethiopian and Syrian — were defined in 1852 in a document known as the Status Quo, which is still in force. The arrangements it determines are of singular complexity, for they refer not only to the parts of the building which belong to each sect, but also to every single object within the Church. Lamps and icons, pillars and walls, chapels and pictures all have their recognised owner who assumes full responsibility for them.

The current restoration of the Church began in 1955 and is still in progress. The patient tap-tap of

the mason's chisels are a familiar sound to all who come within its precincts.

140. Crosses engraved on the wall by mediaeval pilgrims.
141. Throne of the Greek Orthodox Patriarch in the Catholicon.
142. A view over part of the upper gallery and the Arches of the Virgin. The pillars are from the 12th-century Crusader building.
143. The Greek patriarch with his attendants during a colourful religious ceremony at the Sepulchre itself.
144. This pillar is believed to be a fragment of the one to which Jesus was tied when he was flagellated by the Romans. It is in the Franciscan Chapel whose name, the Church of the Apparition, commemorates the apparition of Jesus before his mother Mary.
145. The stone slab known as the Stone of the Anointing. On this stone Christ was laid after his body was taken down from the Cross.
146. This is the altar which stands in the Greek Orthodox Chapel of Golgotha.

146

ΓΕΩΡΓΙΟΣ ΠΡΟΚΟΠ· ΔΗΜΗΤ· ΘΕΟΔΩΡ·Σ ΘΕΟΔΩΡ·Τ ΜΕΡΚΟΥΡ· ΝΙΚΗΤΑΣ ΒΙΚΤΩΡ

147

148

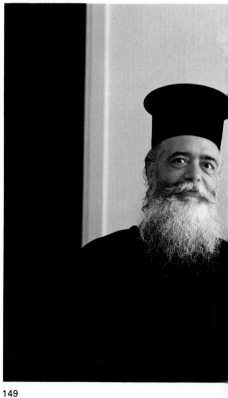

149

The Greek Orthodox community claims descent from the Byzantines who ruled the Holy Land for over three hundred years. In the many upheavals during the Roman and Byzantine periods, the religious centre was moved from Jerusalem to Caesarea and back again, and to Constantinople at the end of the Byzantine Period in the Holy Land. Finally, in the last century, the Greek Orthodox Patriarchate was resettled in Jerusalem, in the Christian Quarter of the Old City. The Custodians of the Greek Orthodox Community watch over their rights and privileges in the Church of the Holy Sepulchre in Jerusalem and the Church of the Nativity in Bethlehem.

The Ethiopians claim that their religious centre was established in Jerusalem from about the eighth century.

They established their monastery on the top of the roof of St. Helena Chapel (151) next to the Church of the Holy Sepulchre, where today, they are in conflict with their neighbours, the Christian Copts, who claim to be the true owners of the place.

150

147. A fresco depicting saints and martyrs. It is in the Crusader refectorium beneath the Greek Orthodox Monastery of St. Abraham near the Holy Sepulchre.
148. A large water reservoir of the Byzantine epoch, or perhaps even earlier, beneath the Monastery of St. Abraham. It is approximately 37 metres long and 13 metres wide.
149. Father Daniel, Custodian of the Greek Orthodox property in the Holy Sepulchre.
150/151. The Ethiopian Monastery on the roof of the Chapel of St. Helena. On the site are remains of a 12th-century Crusader Church which originally belonged to the Augustine monks.

151

152

153

154

Another interesting tradition which concerns the Church of the Holy Sepulchre is the Armenian tradition of the Calvary. According to the Armenian historical records and evidence, today's Calvary which is divided between the Greek Orthodox Church and the Franciscan Fathers, was from the time of Saladin until the middle of the 15th century in Armenian hands. There is continuous evidence of this fact throughout the preceding centuries by many scholars and pilgrims. They mention the different chapels of the Holy Sepulchre and they assign the Calvary to the Armenians.

The earliest mention is by Nicolo of Poggibonsi (1346). Louis de Rochechouart mentions in 1463 that the Armenians are the custodian of a place called "The Calvary." In the latter half of the 15th century we have new information concerning Calvary. It records that, until 1526, it was in Armenian hands and then the Georgians who were related to the Mamelukes by family connections, seized control of it. Finally the Armenians were given the Armenian Gallery, which is today called the Second Golgotha (154).

152. A wooden door in the Armenian Chapel, copy of a 13th-century door from the Armenian monastery of Datuv. The original can be seen in the Armenian Museum in Erevan.
153. The inscription in the Armenian Chapel of the Holy Sepulchre. The cross at the base of the plaque commemorates Peter and his parents.
154. A mosaic in the Armenian Chapel, depicting the birth of Jesus. It was designed after an illustration by Gouros Roslin in a 12th-century Armenian edition of the New Testament.
155/156. The skull-shaped rock in the Garden Tomb, or Gordon's Calvary.

The Garden Tomb (156) is believed by Protestants to be the true burial place of Jesus — not the Holy Sepulchre revered by the Roman Catholics and the Greek Orthodox. It lies beneath a rise which supposedly resembles a human skull — Golgotha in Aramaic. It is also known as Gordon's Calvary, after the reknowned British general, "Chinese" Charles Gordon, who visited Jerusalem in 1883 and became convinced that this was the true tomb of Jesus.

Immediately adjacent to the Garden Tomb were found traces of the Church of St. Stephen which, according to the Christian belief, was the burial place of this first Christian martyr.

155

156

157

158

159

The Crusader church of St. Anne's, not far from the Lions' Gate, is named after the mother of Mary and grandmother of Jesus. In the 5th century, a Byzantine church dedicated to St. Mary was erected on the site by Eudocia. Though destroyed by the Persians in 614, it was rebuilt shortly afterwards. Six hundred years later, the Crusaders built a new church just south-east of the Byzantine structure, and to this day the 12th-century building has preserved the austere beauty typical of the architecture of that period. The Crusaders also rededicated the church to St. Anne.

After the defeat of the Crusaders at the Battle of the Horns of Hittin in 1187, Saladin transformed the church into a Moslem school, and for seven hundred years the building remained in Moslem hands. In the 19th century the Turkish Sultan Abdul el-Majjid turned it over to the French as a gesture of gratitude for their support in the Crimean War.

Looking up carefully at the façade of St. Anne's, one can see that part of the building leans slightly over to the side. This was an architectural form commonly used in France to symbolise the Crucifixion.

Next to St. Anne's Church is the Pool of Bethesda. Christians identify it with the pool mentioned in the Gospel according to St. John (5:2), where Jesus is said to have performed the miracle of the healing. The pool's curative properties were known to the Romans in the 3rd and 4th centuries A.D. and for generations Christians came to bathe in its healing waters.

The pool is divided into two reservoirs, the construction apparently dating from the days of the Maccabees. Archaeological excavations on the site revealed pottery and coins from Hasmonean times in the second century B.C. until the year 66 B.C.

157. The lintel of the eastern entrance to the Crusader church of St. Anne's is engraved with this Byzantine cross.
158. Saladin's Arabic inscription above the entrance to the Church of St. Anne.
159. The southern reservoir of the Pool of Bethesda. Remains of the foundations of the Byzantine church continue down to the bottom of the pool, while above them are traces of both the Byzantine and Crusader churches.
160. Ancient remains found in the excavations in the cloister of the Church of St. Anne.
161. Details of a Byzantine pedestal engraved with the Byzantine cross. On it stands the base of a column which probably embellished the nave of the Basilica of Eudocia.
162. To the left of the Crusader church and in the background are the ruins of the Byzantine church, and the southern Pool of Bethesda.

160

161

162

Jerusalem holds a privileged place in the hearts of Christians everywhere. Names such as the Mount of Olives, the Garden of Gethsemane, the Via Dolorosa and Golgotha never fail to evoke the scenes and events described by the Apostles. On all the sites associated with the Passion and death of Jesus, churches have been erected, indeed, in some places several shrines have been set around the same spot.

Perhaps the most impressive is the Church of Mary Magdalene, (164), a cluster of onion domes nestling in the Garden of Gethsemane. Built in 1888 by Czar Alexander III in memory of his mother, the church is typical of 17th-century Russian design. At night, illuminated (165), it looks for all the world like a princely wedding cake.

The diagonal bar on the crosses surmounting the towers (163) sym-

163

164

bolises the resurrection. In fact, the tomb of Elisabeth Feodorovna, sister of the last Czar of Russia, lies in the crypt below. With her husband, Duke Serge of Moscow, she was among the founders of the Imperial Orthodox Society of Palestine. The Duchess met a violent death during the Russian revolution but her sister knew of her desire to be buried in this church, and in 1921, the "White" Russians contrived to bring her remains to Jerusalem — via Peking!

The church, with its accompanying monastery, belongs to the "White" Russian Orthodox sect, whose centre is now in the United States. Vereshaguine and Ivanoff painted the pictures which decorate the interior.

In the monastery courtyard are the remains of an ancient flight of steps, perhaps the one mentioned in 9th-century Latin documents, which describe the entrance to Jerusalem from the east by way of 537 steps down the Mount of Olives to the Valley of Kidron, and 195 leading from the Valley up to St. Stephen's Gate.

At the foot of the Russian compound rises the Church of All Nations (166), its façade glowing among the silvery green trees of Gethsemane. In ancient times this was the site of an oil press for the olives grown nearby, as its Hebrew name, *Gat Shemanim*, meaning oil press, shows. Some of the olive trees in the Garden may be as much as two thousand years old. It was in this tranquil haven

163/164/166. The Muscovite onion domes on the Russian Church of Mary Magadalene.
165. The Mary Magadalene Church at night.

166

that Jesus was wont to sit with his disciples, and it was from here that he was led away to prison by the Roman guards.

The site was first consecrated by the early Byzantine Christians, and traces of their 5th-century church can still be seen. After the destruction of the first church by invaders, a second one was built by the Crusaders in the 12th century, only to be destroyed in its turn by the Moslem conquerors. The site remained deserted until 1919 when work on the present edifice began. It owes its name to the fact that men of all nations contributed to its construction.

The church's brilliant mosaic (169) depicts Jesus as the link between Man and his Creator, with the whole of humanity raising their eyes to him in hope. Above his head appear the Greek letters Alpha and Omega, as it is said in Revelation 1:8: " 'I am Alpha and Omega, the Beginning and the Ending,' saith the Lord." On the pillars stand statues of the four

167

Evangelists: Matthew, Mark, Luke and John. The deer which face the cross surmounting the façade symbolise David's eloquent verse: "As the hart panteth after the water brooks, so panteth my soul after Thee, O God" (Psalms, 42:2).

The Church of the Assumption (172) marks the spot where Mary is believed to have been buried.

Her body was brought there from Mt. Zion and, according to Christian tradition, it is from here that she rose to Heaven. The present church was built by the Crusaders on the site of an earlier shrine, and is one of the rare examples of 12th-century architecture which have survived intact. The entrance is in pure romanesque style. It is

168

169

70

171

graced with pointed archways supported by slender pillars whose capitals are embellished with Crusader-style leaf pattern.

The Church of the Assumption belongs to the Greek Orthodox Church, but is shared with the Armenians and the Copts. Flank-

167/169. A view of the deer and the illustrated mosaics of the Church of All Nations.
168. An old olive tree in the Garden of Gethsemane.
170. A Crusader portal of the Church of Mary.
171. The outer passage-way of the Church of Mary.
172. The Church of Mary.

172

173

174

175

176

177

ing the stairs which lead down to Mary's tomb are what some believe to be the tombs of her parents, Yehoachim and Hannah.

This graceful edifice marks the grave of Moudjire-Din el Hanbali (176), a 16th-century Moslem jurist renowned for his scholarly works on the Holy City. The cupola, with its shell-like moulding, is set upon four pillars which give the monument its airy elegance.

It is from the site of this lovely shrine (179) atop the Mount of Olives that Jesus is said to have ascended to Heaven. Beneath the dome lies a stone bearing a footprint which, according to tradition, was left by the Master as He rose from the earth. The Church of the Ascension, as it is called, bears the traces of earlier structures: its octagonal base, whose pillars support a drum, is reminiscent of Crusader architecture, which sometimes drew its inspiration from Byzantine forms; the cupola is of Moslem style, for at one time the church served as a mosque; as for the circular courtyard surrounding the shrine, it was added in 1835 on the remains of the 12th-century Crusader church which was destroyed during the Moslem conquest. Around it are altars belonging to different Christian sects.

173. The belfry in the courtyard of the Church of the Assumption.
174/175. Bells and decorations at the entrance to the Church of the Assumption.
176. The grave of Moudjire-Din el Hanabli.
177. The interior of the Church of the Assumption. A Greek Orthodox priest is standing beside Mary's tomb.
178. The Church of the Dominus Flevit.
179. The Church of the Ascension.

178

179

180

181

The triptych above the entrance to St. Mark's Syrian Orthodox Church (181) is a graphic description of the events traditionally associated with this ancient holy place. The left panel shows Peter's release from prison by the angels and his flight to Mark's house which is believed to have stood on the site. The middle picture depicts the gathering of Mary and the Apostles there after Jesus's resurrection, the third one shows Peter arriving at Mark's house after the Last Supper.

The 6th-century A.D. inscription on the plaque in the northern wall of the church is in Aramaic (180). the language still used by the Syrian Orthodox sect. It relates: "This is the house of Mary, mother of John called Mark. Proclaimed a church by the Holy Apostles under the name of the Virgin Mary, mother of God, after the ascension of our Lord Jesus Christ into Heaven. Built after the destruction of Jerusalem by Titus in the year 73 A.D.".

The Orthodox Syrians are one of the oldest Christian sects, claiming descent from Abraham. Their church, a 12th-century Crusader structure standing on the foundations of earlier buildings, lies between the Armenian and the Jewish Quarters.

One of the charms of Jerusalem is the architectural variety it offers. In the heart of the bustling modern capital outside the Old City walls, one suddenly comes upon a 19th-century Russian Cathedral (183), its graceful green domes set, not in their customary snowbound landscape, but under Jerusalem's brilliant sun. The cathedral, built in 1860 by the Russian Orthodox Palestine Society, was conceived as part of a compound designed to cater for the many Russian pilgrims in Jerusalem. The Compound also contained a hospital, living quarters, and one building was and is used as a jail until today. The entire area — some 60,000 square metres — was surrounded by a solid wall which protected it from the marauders who roamed Jerusalem at the turn of the century. The buildings which the Church authorities no longer use are rented by the Israel Government.

182

180. The Aramaic inscription in the Syrian Orthodox Church of St. Mark.
181. The entrance to the Syrian Orthodox Church of St. Mark, with the triptych depicting events from the New Testament.
182. The ancient Russian Orthodox insignia.
183. The roofs of the Russian Cathedral, with its green domes against the blue Mediterranean sky.

183

184

To enter the Armenian compound (185), one must pass through a heavy iron gateway on which an Armenian inscription reads: "This gate was built by the Patriarch Krikor in the year 1646." The marble drinking fountain in the courtyard dates from the turn of the century. It bears the following wish: "May all who drink in this place have a thought for the anonymous builder."

The Armenian nation has its origins in Armenia in the southern Caucasus — biblical Ararat, according to tradition — today a Republic of the Soviet Union. It was Saint Gregory who, in the 3rd century, brought Christianity to that region, hence the Armenian Church's other name, the Gregorian Church. Most of the 3,500 Armenians who live in Jerusalem today are Gregorians. They speak their own language, of Indo-Euro-

186

187

185

188

pean derivation, and lead an active cultural life which helps them preserve their identity. They even have their own printing press. Many Armenians are members of the free professions; others engage in arts and crafts, particularly ceramics and jewellery.

The Armenian museum contains works of art of inestimable value, while the library, named after the Armenian oil tycoon Gulbenkian, who contributed a vast sum of money to its construction in 1929, houses manuscripts the like of which are rarely seen.

The site of the Armenian Cathedral of St. James (196) is believed

184. *The Old City street in which the Armenian Patriarchate stands is marked by this picturesque street sign — a foretaste of the exceptional things to come.*
185. *The entrance to the courtyard of the Armenian monastery is faced with stone. In the foreground is the guardian's room, to the right the drinking fountain, and to the left an iron door.*
186. *Archbishop Norair Bogharian is the librarian of the magnificent Armenian collection. Here he is reading from the 1337 Armenian edition of the Book of the Four Gospels.*
187. *Detail of the* khatchkar *stone cross set into the wall of the Armenian convent. Khatchkars, marble plaques or stones engraved with crosses and Armenian inscriptions, were put up by pilgrims. The oldest known in Jerusalem dates from 1151.*
188. *An Armenian tombstone.*
189. *Detail of the 12th century Gospel of St. Luke in the Armenian Book of the Four Gospels, from the Hromkla Library.*
190. *The Four Gospels of Lady Keran, copyist and painter: another manuscript dated 1265 from the Hromkla Library of St. Thoros.*
191. *This is an Armenian book dated 1265, from the Hromkla Library of St. Thoros. The illustration depicts the Harrowing of Hell and is the work of the artist Thoros-Roslin.*

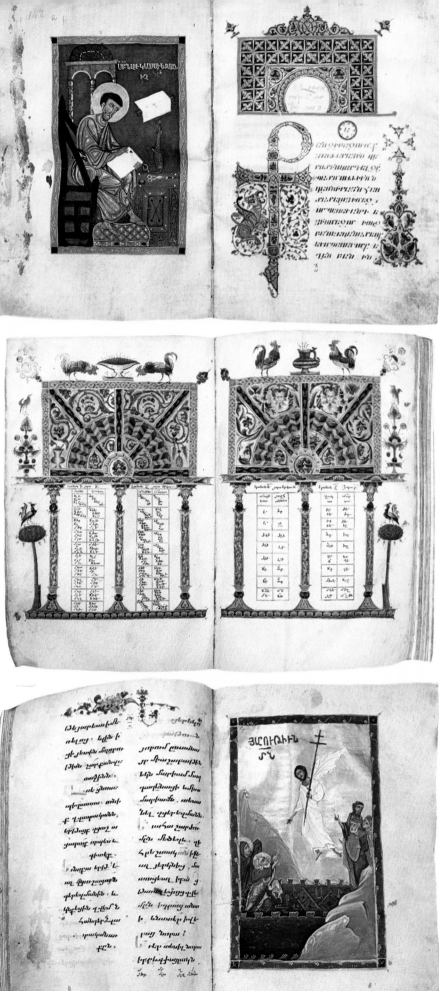

189

190

191

to be the place where James the Apostle, brother of John the Evangelist, was put to death by Herod Agrippa in 44 A.D. It was founded in the 5th century but destroyed two hundred years later by the Persians, together with all the other Christian edifices in Jerusalem. The present structure was built in the 11th century and has not changed much since. Near the entrance hangs a wooden plank The Armenians sound it to call the faithful to prayer, a custom they have preserved since the times when the Moslems prohibited Christians from ringing their church bells.

On the 10th of January, St. James's Day, the old church takes on a festive air, and the sunlight, filtering in through the high windows of the dome, suffuses it with an aura of sanctity. Some of the most precious Armenian treasures are taken out for the occasion, among them the mitre (194) worn by the Patriarch during the liturgy. Fashioned in 1740 for Gregory the Chainbearer, it is studded with many precious stones, and its elaborate embroidery is renowned the world over.

192

193

194

195

196

In honour of the day, a special altar is erected (193). On it ancient ritual objects from the Armenian collection are put on display, but immediately after the ceremony they are removed for safety. Among objects shown here are chalices, crosses and ostensoria. All the vessels are set with precious stones and many are the work of highly skilled Armenian craftsmen. Most of the lamps and ritual objects were presented to the church by the Armenian goldsmiths of Istanbul and Isphahan.

192. A splendid embroidered curtain depicting Mary holding James's head after he had been decapitated.
193. Chalices and symbolic dove representing the Holy Ghost placed on the altar of St. James.
194. Mitre of Patriarch Gregory the Chainbearer which is worn only on very special occasions.
195/196. (Above left): An Armenian monk. (Above right): A shaft of sunlight pierces the gloom, illuminating the numerous oil-lamps.
197. Figures in Armenian Kutahya style ceramics. Many antique pieces can be seen in the church.
198. This is a unique example of Armenian ceramics. Its delicate decorations, depicting scenes from the Old and New Testaments, are based on illuminations in mediaeval manuscripts.

197

198

199

200

201

202

203

204

The Monastery of the Cross (202) is one of the beauties of Jerusalem, nestling in the valley between the residential suburb of Rehavia and Israel's national Museum. It owes its name to the belief that the tree from which the cross of Jesus was fashioned grew on the valley's wooded slopes.

Who built the Monastery of the Cross is not known. Some say that it was the work of the 5th-century Georgian king Tatian, who erected it on land that had been presented as a gift to Marian, the first Christian king of Georgia, some years earlier. Others ascribe it to Constantine and Helena, as they built so many of the religious edifices in Jerusalem. Justinian is recorded as having restored the Georgian monastery in Jerusalem, and though it is not mentioned by name, it is assumed to be the Monastery of the Cross. The first mention of it in Greek documents dates from the 6th century.

A fascinating legend attaches itself to the Monastery. It is that after Valerius, Commander of Justinian's armies, had conquered

Rome, he took possession of the ritual vessels which had been brought there as trophies from the Second Temple, and had them returned to Jerusalem. At first he placed them in the Nea Basilica but later, for fear they might fall into the hands of his enemies should he lose the city, he had them transferred for safe-keeping to the Monastery of the Cross. To make doubly sure, the monks buried them. However, in 796, under Moslem rule, all the inhabitants of the monastery were massacred and no one survived to reveal the hiding place of the priceless vessels.

Pilgrims began to visit the Monastery of the Cross during Crusader times, and all their accounts describe its singular beauty.

The monastery was destroyed in the reign of Bibars and was turned into a mosque, but thanks to the good offices of the ruler of Constantinople in early 14th century, it was restored to the Georgians. The Moslems later demanded its restitution, but in vain, and the Monastery remained in Christian hands. It changed ownership

in the 17th century when the Greek Orthodox Church took it over, and has remained in its possession. Until 1903, the Monastery served as a theological seminary for visiting priests, and in recent years has been used as a hospice.

In 1960 a special delegation of scientists from the Soviet Republic of Georgia came to Israel to investigate the Monastery of the Cross. They hoped to find early Georgian artifacts and manuscripts, especially of the Georgian national poet, Shota Rustavelli, who died here, in the 12th century. But they were disappointed.

199. A monk of the Monastery of the Cross.
200. A view of the upper part of the belfry.
201. The belfry in the courtyard of the Monastery of the Cross.
202. A view of the Monastery.
203. Early frescoes on pillars in the Monastery church.
204. At night, the Monastery of the Cross takes on an almost ethereal quality. Subtle illuminations give its solid contours a grace and lightness, echoed by the delicate form of the National Museum, which lies beyond.

205

Just north-west of Jerusalem, the tranquil village of Ein Karem clings to the Judaean hillside, its low-lying houses dwarfed by the tapering cypresses which rise from the slopes. Some scholars believe that today's Ein Karem corresponds to the Bet Hakerem mentioned in the Bible. Curiously, though it lay within the territory allotted to the tribe of Judah, it is not explicitly mentioned in the biblical description of that area, yet it did come through in the form of Cherem in the Greek Sep-

tuagint. Jeremiah's warning of an attack on Judaea from the north was made in these terms: "And set up a sign of fire in Beth-haccerem, for evil appeareth out of the north and great destruction" (Jeremiah 6:1). The site is not named in the New Testament either, but there is an ancient Christian tradition that the "city of Judaea" to which the Gospel refers is in fact Ein Karem.

Ein Karem is sacred to Christians because John the Baptist, son of Elisabeth and Zacharia, is

206

thought to have been born there. Zacharia himself belonged to the priestly sect which served in the Second Temple at the beginning of the first century A.D.

The mosaic on the façade of the Church of the Visitation shows the Virgin Mary and Jesus riding on a donkey from Nazareth to visit the family of John the Baptist at their summer house in Ein Karem — hence the church's name. Nazareth, and the road leading from it to Ein Karem, are shown at the left of the picture. Beneath it is a Latin inscription from Luke 1:39: "Exurgens autem Maria in diebus illis abiit in montana cum festinatione, in civitatem Juda." "And Mary arose in those days, and went into the hill country with haste, into a city of Judaea."

The Church of the Visitation (206) commands a delightful view over the valley below. It belongs to the Franciscan friars and is near the place where the home of John the Baptist and his family is thought to have stood. It has two storeys. To the outer walls of the lower storey ancient hewn stones are affixed, while the interior houses paintings of Mary's visit, the High Priest Zacharia, and Roman soldiers hounding mothers and babes. Christian tradition relates that when the Romans came in search of John, he disappeared miraculously into the stone which is kept in a special cell within the church.

The upper storey contains a vast prayer hall decorated with pictures illustrating scenes from the history of Christianity. Among the scenes is the Marriage at Cana (the Galilean Kfar Kana), where the first miracle of Jesus — the transformation of water into wine — is said to have taken place.

Within the building are vestiges of a two-storied Crusader church. Inevitably it fell into decay after the expulsion of the European knights, and apart from the courtyard which was inhabited by Moslems, not much of it has survived. In 1679 the Franciscans purchased the ruins, but it was not until 1862 that they restored the place and built the lower storey of the present church. The upper was added in 1955. Excavations carried out in 1937 revealed remains going back to the Romans.

MAGNIFICAT

My soul magnifies the Lord, and my spirit rejoices in God my Savior. Because He has regarded the lowliness of His handmaid. For behold, henceforth all generations shall call me blessed, because He who is mighty has done great things for me, and Holy is His name, and for generation upon generation is His mercy to those who fear Him. He has shown might with His arm. He has scattered the proud in the conceit of their heart. He has put down the mighty from their thrones, and has exalted the lowly. He has filled the hungry with good things, and the rich He has sent away empty. He has given help to Israel his servant. Mindful of His mercy — even as He spoke to our fathers — to Abraham and to his posterity forever.

205. A window in the Church of the Visitation.
206. A view of the entrance to the church courtyard. Over the gates rise the statues of Elisabeth and Zacharia, the golden cross between them glittering in the sunshine.
207/212. Mary's prayer to Elisabeth, known as the Magnificat, is inscribed in forty-two languages on ceramic plaques affixed to one of the walls of the church courtyard.

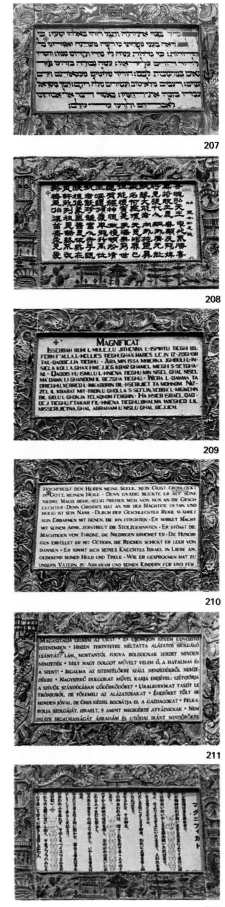

207

208

209

210

211

212

The Dome of the Rock (213), its golden cupola resplendent on its gleaming blue base, rests like a jewel on the heart of Jerusalem. Beside it, so that it should not stand unaccompanied in its majesty, the silver dome of El Aqsa shimmers in the sunshine.

The Temple Mount, on which these edifices stand, has a recorded history of nearly four thousand years. It is first mentioned in an early Egyptian Execration Text of the 19th-18th century B.C. The Patriarch Abraham met its king, Malchizedek (Genesis 14:18), and it is traditionally identified as Mount Moriah, where Isaac was to be sacrificed to God. King David captured it from the Jebusites, promising to erect upon it an altar and a sanctuary to the Jews' One God. The fulfilment of this vow was left to his son, and in 955 B.C. Solomon's wondrous Temple was completed. The Babylonians destroyed it in 586 B.C., but it was rebuilt by Ezra and Nehemiah on their return from exile. The Second Temple was severely damaged by the Seleucid invaders and yet again restored, this time by the Hasmonean dynasty. A century later, King Herod embarked on a major reconstruction both of the esplanade and the sanctuary itself, enlarging and embellishing both. The results, according to contemporary descriptions was one of the most splendid edifices the world had ever seen. After the destruction of the Temple and pal-

ace at the hands of Titus' legions in 70 A.D., the Mount remained desolate. Hadrian's symbolic attempt to erect a temple to Jupiter on the site in 130 A.D. set off the last Jewish revolt led by Bar Kokhba. In the 4th-century, the Byzantine Emperor Julian "the Apostate" gave the Jews permission to rebuild the Temple, but the project died with him.

The Mount, known in Arabic as Haram esh Sharif — the Noble Sanctuary — was a scene of desola-

tion until the end of the 7th century when the Omayyad Caliph Abd el Malik ibn Merwan erected the Dome of the Rock upon it. As its name implies, the building stands on the rock, where according to Jewish tradition, the Holy

213. A view of the Dome of the Rock. In the background are the churches of the Mount of Olives.
214. The upper portion of a Mameluke façade on the esplanade. The building is named after Sheik Mohammed al-Halil whose tomb is inside.

215. The finely-decorated dome of the Sabil Qait Bey, a drinking fountain built by the Mameluke Sultan Qait in 1482, and restored in 1883 by the Turkish Sultan Abdul Hamid. From it steps lead up to the Dome of the Rock.
216. The Arcade of the Scales is one of several which stand at the top of the stairs leading from the esplanade up to the Dome of the Rock. Arabic inscriptions on them indicate that they were built during the 14th century in Mameluke times. However, most of the pillars and capitals came from earlier constructions.
217. A view over the Temple Mount from the Dome of the Rock.

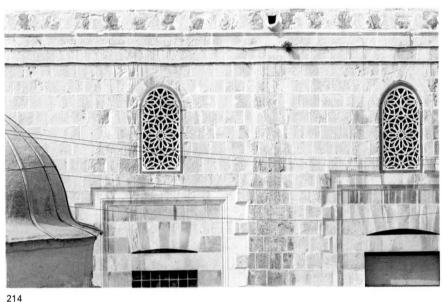

214

215

216

217

Ark was laid. The Moslems, for their part, believe that it was from here that Mohammed ascended to heaven. The Dome of the Rock is a sacred shrine in Islam. It is often, mistakenly, called the Mosque of Omar, after the Caliph in whose reign the Holy Land was brought under Moslem rule. Caliph Omar prayed near the rock in 638, sixty years before the shrine was built.

The Dome of the Rock is set on the highest point of the beautifully paved plateau which has, in the main, retained its original Herodian dimensions. Steps lead up to the shrine from all directions, delicate arcades standing at the head of each flight. The building is of

218. A glimpse of the Dome of the Chain.

218

219

20

221

219. A view towards the Dome of the Rock.

221. A devout Arab bathing his feet at the Elcas a ritual washing and drinking fountain. The circular construction has a series of taps running around it, and stone seats are provided for the comfort of the believers.

220/222. An Arab sun-dial set into the Arcade of the Scales at the southern entrance to the Dome of the Rock. It was built in Ottoman times for the Moslems who came to pray on the Temple Mount.

222

223

224

octagonal form, and its outer walls are faced with a rich combination of marble and blue ceramic tiles. Along its upper border runs a long Arabic quotation from Chapter 39 of the Koran (223).

The Dome of the Rock was built by the Caliph Abd el Malik, of the Omayyad dynasty, at the end of the seventh century. Did he wish to divert the flow of Moslem pilgrims from Mecca to Jerusalem (and, incidentally, reduce the influence of his rival, Abdallah Ibn Zubair of Mecca), or did he set out to create a Moslem shrine in Jerusalem to counter-balance the Holy Sepulchre? In any event, it is important to remember that in those days the Arabic name for Jerusalem was still *Beit al Maqdas* ("The Temple"), and the location and magnificence of the Dome of the Rock were undoubtedly designed to recall the lost glory of the Judaean kingdom.

Abd el-Malik had the interior of the shrine embellished with mosaics into which an Arabic inscription bearing his name, his titles and the date of the mosque's construction was worked. However, when sovereignty over Jerusalem passed to the Abassid dynasty, his name was removed and that of the Abassid Caliph Abdullah Ha'aman el-Mamun inserted in its place. Curiously, the new ruler forgot to alter the date — and so the inscription has remained to this day.

At the eastern entrance of the Dome of the Rock stands the Dome of the Chain (218), which is a diminutive model of it. According to legend, King David used to sit in Judgement here. Near it, we are told, hung a chain which the accused had to grasp. If he lied, a link fell from it and his guilt was

225

226

revealed. The Dome of the Chain was built in the 8th century to house the Moslem treasures on the Temple Mount. The Crusaders converted it into a chapel in memory of St. James, the first bishop of Jerusalem, but in 16th-century Ottoman times Suleiman the Magnificent had the building restored and tiled with ceramics.

223-225. The southern entrance to the Dome of the Rock is sometimes called the "Gate of Prayer" and is not used today. Above the entrance is an inscription from the Koran commanding the believers to pray towards Mecca. The Arabic inscriptions are not only used to convey a religious message, but also as artistic decorations. On the right one can see a marble image of two birds, believed to have been turned to stone for disobeying King Solomon.
226. A series of elaborately decorated windows and panels.
227. A decorated marble panel on the outer wall of the Dome.
228. A window grille in the Dome.

227   228

229

231

230

The Dome of the Rock is one of the few surviving creations of the magnificent Omayyad dynasty. No one who enters it can fail to be amazed and moved by its extraordinary beauty. The wealth of ornamentation defies the eye. Here certain classical elements are blended into the vibrant new artistic concepts of the emerging Islamic civilization. Geometric and floral motifs, colours and forms express the dynamic force of a nascent culture, rapidly spreading from the Indian Ocean to the Atlantic.

With the penchant for the gorgeous and magnificent moderated by the religious tendency to austerity, with the immense wealth of the newly conquered lands, the Caliph Abd el Malik created a rare masterpiece.

'32

233

229. *The interior arches of the Dome of the Rock are embellished with various motifs. The upper register, which divides the columns from the Dome itself, is split by a narrow band of floral design, typical to the Holy Land in the Byzantine period (5th to 7th centuries A.D.).*

230. *In addition to an internal row of columns, the Dome is also supported by an external row of pillars and columns, which, in turn, support a decorative architrave and arches of vegetation.*

231. *Another interesting pattern, found in the lower portion of the Dome, is a series of amphoras, with scrolls of vegetation from their mouths.*

232. *The inside of the Dome is adorned with the* arabesque *design in stucco, with a strong colour — gold on a red background. In contrast, the other patterns are floral motifs executed in glass mosaic.*

233. *A metal decorative band, bearing a palmetto and grape motif.*

234. *The inside of the Dome, with its gold chain falling to the centre of the world.*

234

235

at the end of the 7th century. The earthquakes and natural catastrophes which struck Jerusalem were no kinder to it than to the rest of the city's structures. Its present form dates from 1033 when it was restored by Caliph El Zahir. Under the Crusaders El Aqsa was used as a palace for the European kings. It remained in the hands of the Knights Templar until Saladin's victory and the return of Moslem sovereignty over Jerusalem. Then the mosque was redecorated in rich Moslem style.

The most striking feature of El Aqsa is its spacious interior, its loftiness recalling the great cathedrals of Christendom. It contains no furniture whatsoever, the austerity relieved only by the scores of precious carpets which cover the floor, donated by Moslems from all over the world.

The silver-domed mosque of El Aqsa stands on the extreme southern edge of the Temple Mount, just above one of the underground passages which in Second Temple times, led from the Hulda Gates up to the Temple Mount. In Arabic its name means "the remote mosque," and it is generally believed to be the "farthest mosque" mentioned in the Koran. Farthest, that is, from Mecca, for Mecca is the centre of Islam, and El Aqsa takes third place among the great mosques of Islam, after Mecca and Medina.

El Aqsa was constructed by Abd el Malik or his son Al Walid

236

Until recently entrance to El Aqsa was barred to non-Moslems.

"Solomon's Stables," beneath the south-eastern corner of the Temple Mount, were probably built by Herod to reinforce the retaining wall of the compound and the foundation of the Temple; the gradient of the bedrock is particularly steep at this point. Christians believe that this was where Mary rested the cradle of Jesus (237) when she came to the Temple to pray. The Templars used the place as stables for the Crusader cavalry.

235. The façade of El Aqsa.
236. El Aqsa as seen from Mt. Zion, with the Mount of Olives in the background.
237/239. The interior of "Solomon's Stables."
238. The window at the south-east corner of "Solomon's Stables," near the "Cradle of Jesus."

237

238

239

240

241

In the semi-desert of the Middle East, natural water sources are more precious than all the other necessities of life. From the dawn of history, the inhabitants of the region learned to store the precious liquid, and devised ways of preventing it from evaporating. Despite its turbulent history, Jerusalem itself never lacked for water — its springs and man-made wells and pools always proved adequate in time of peace as in time of war.

The Gihon Springs, the oldest known water source in Jerusalem, gushes forth in the Kidron Valley, south-west of the Pillar of Absalom. Its waters come from the nearby western hills where rainfall is plentiful, and spurt intermittently under pressure when the passages to it are filled.

Being the principal source on the Judaean watershed, the Gihon spring attracted both the Amorites and the Jebusites, who established their settlements nearby. Archaeological excavations indicate that it was probably the Jebusites who sank a shaft to the bottom of the pool in order to provide direct access to it from the city itself, a factor of prime importance in wartime.

The Gihon was considered holy in ancient times: King Solomon was anointed beside it, and the New Testament relates that there Jesus made the blind man see.

Originally the water of the Gihon was drawn directly, but as time went by it was allowed to collect in the Siloam pool, so as to be more easily accessible to the inhabitants of the city. When Sennacherib marched on Jerusalem, Hezekiah, King of Judah,

42

243

dug a conduit through the hillside by which the water of the Gihon was brought within the city. A Hebrew inscription inside the tunnel commemorated the point where the workmen, digging from both ends, met. But Hezekiah also blocked the outlet of the source that lay outside the city walls, and diverted the water to a pool which he constructed within Jerusalem's fortifications. Thus he not only ensured an adequate supply of water for his people, but also deprived his enemies of it. (II Kings 20:20, Chronicles 32:2—4 and Isaiah 22:11.)

The Israelites were skillful well-diggers. Because of the pre-

240. The Pool of the Towers (Hezekiah), probably built in the Second Temple period.
241. One of Solomon's Pools which supplied water to Jerusalem.
242. Water flowing from a conduit from the Pool of Siloam.
243. The Upper Aqueduct which carried water from Solomon's Pools to Jerusalem.
244. The entrance to the Spring of Gihon.

carious military situation of Jerusalem, a city of solid rocks, scanty rainfall and meagre water resources, they conceived the idea of sinking wells within their dwellings, plastering them, and using them to store rainwater. Special reservoirs were built around the Temple Mount for the many pilgrims who thronged to it.

Perhaps it was their wanderings in the wilderness which taught the Israelites to collect water in pools, a technique which could easily be applied in the hill country of Jerusalem. There were a few score man-made pools in Jerusalem in Second Temple times, one of the better-known being the so-called Sultan's Pool, probably the Snake's Pool mentioned by Josephus in the first century A.D. The pool was rebuilt by Suleiman the Magnificent in 1536, and on the dam stands a lovely drinking fountain whose construction is commemo-

rated on the elaborate inscription it bears. The Pool of the Towers was near Jaffa Gate and may have supplied Herod's palace, as well as the towers which protected them.

The great expansion of the city of Jerusalem in Herodian times made an increased water supply imperative. To solve the problem, a complex system of aqueducts was built through which the waters of the Hebron hills and Solomon's pools were collected, and led down by gravity to Jerusalem. These conduits supplied Jerusalem for centuries, and their remains can be seen today all over the hills between Jerusalem and Hebron.

Even from later historical records we can infer that at least one of the aqueducts continued to supply water to the city of Jerusalem until the present time. An inscription from the Byzantine period has been found, which states that it was forbidden for farmers

245

246

247

and peasants to plant and to seed
within a distance of 15 feet from
the aqueduct. Anyone who dared
to go against this decree was liable
to the death penalty and his property was confiscated.

A Christian pilgrim who visited
Jerusalem in the Omayyad period,
described a bridge built with
arches and upon it an aqueduct,
which spanned the Valley of Hin-
nom near the Pool of the Sultan.
Even in the Middle Ages aqueducts remained in use and supplied water from the hills of Hebron to Solomon's Pools and from
there to Jerusalem. In the Ottoman period the Turks repaired the
aqueduct and even after the
British conquest of Palestine in
1917 the aqueduct still served Jerusalem.

*245. A water cistern with an engraved
inscription in the Armenian Convent,
utilizing subterranean sources.*
*246. The Siloam Pool at the mouth
of Hezekiah's Tunnel.*
*247. An old water-pump which was in
use in modern times.*
*248. A detail of the water fountain in
the Muristan Square.*
*249. A Turkish Sabil (drinking
fountain) from the 16th century near
the "Sultan's Pool."*
*250. A general view of the fountain in
the Muristan Square.*

249

248

250

251

252

251. The spire of Saint Salvador Monastery. It belongs to the Franciscan order, whose centre is not far from the New Gate. In 1342, Pope Clement VI entrusted the Franciscans with the custody of the Holy Land, a privilege which is theirs to this day.

252. The Italian Hospital, its mediaeval Italian style recalling Florence and Sienna, was built during World War I.

253. The Moslem qadi who is responsible for the grounds of the Church of the Ascension.

254. To the left, the spire of the Pater Noster Church; to the right, the dome of the Ascension Mosque beside the Church by the same name. Herodion can be seen in the background.

The original edifice of the Pater Noster Church, built by Constantine, was erected over the grotto where, according to Christian tradition, Jesus taught his disciples the Lord's Prayer. The church is also called "Eleona," which means "of the olive trees" in Greek, and "supreme" in Hebrew. It was destroyed and rebuilt several times before it was finally purchased in 1868 by the Princesse de la Tour d'Auvergne. The Carmelite Order built the present-day church and convent.

253

254

255

In the 19th century, the Germans, following the example of the British and the French, sought ways of obtaining political influence in the Holy Land by means of religious activity. They succeeded in establishing a proper German colony in the country. One of their most ambitious projects was an orphanage for Syrian children, whose parents had perished in the massacres of Christians. Named after its founder Ludwig Schneller, the complex was built between 1856 and 1900 out of contributions made by the German Protestants. It was composed of a number of buildings over a wide area, the most impressive among them being the clock-tower building (255) in which the children lived. The others housed workshops where the orphans were taught a trade: there was a tile factory used, incidentally, by the children to bake their clay; a shoemaker's, a blacksmith's, a potter's corner and other facilities. A school for the blind was also established in 1903, and teachers' residences were built along the street outside the compound. "Schneller," as the site came to be known, was turned into a German army camp during

256

World War I, and was taken over by the British forces following the German defeat. Today it is used by the Israel Defence Forces.

The tower of Augusta Victoria (257), standing at 830 metres above sea level, on the crest of the watershed between the Jordan Valley and the Mediterranean Sea, is an outstanding landmark on Jerusalem's eastern hills. It is named after the wife of Wilhelm II of Germany, who laid the cornerstone during the visit of the royal couple to Jerusalem in 1898. Augusta Victoria was originally built as a hospice for German pilgrims, and the church beside it is known as the Church of the Ascension of Jesus to Heaven. After the British conquest of Jerusalem in 1917, the hospice was converted into the residence of the British High Commissioner. Here Herbert Samuel, the first person to hold that title, celebrated the marriage of his son Edwin, the present Viscount Samuel. The building was damaged in the 1927 earthquake and after its repair, turned into a hospital. Between 1948 and 1967 it lay unused in the zone under United Nations control. Since the reunification of Jerusalem in 1967, it has been functioning as a hospital once again, with the financial support of the World Lutheran Society.

The slender tower of the Y.M.C.A. (258) is one of the most decorative in Jerusalem. For years it has served as a landmark for the tens of thousands of tourists who visit the city each year, and from its top a magnificent panorama of

255. The Gothic Clock-Tower at Schneller's.
256. The pediment of the Schneller building.
257. The Augusta Victoria Hospital.

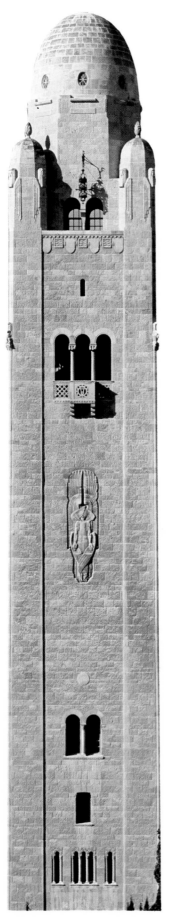

the city can be seen. Work on the Y.M.C.A. building began in 1928, and it was inaugurated five years later. The principal endorsement came from the American James Newbegin Jarvie, and its architect was none other than Q. L. Harmon, the designer of the Empire State Building in New York.

Today the Y.M.C.A. serves as a community centre for all the inhabitants of Israel's capital, Jews and Arabs. It provides sports facilities, a library, an archaeological exhibition and accommodation for visitors. There is another Y.M.C.A. building in the eastern part of the city, but it is not nearly as magnificent as this.

When the foundations of the building were being laid, remains of a monastery and ancient graves were revealed and a 6th-century Greek inscription. The top of the tower is decorated with the legendary figures of seraphim inspired by Isaiah's vision: "Above him stood the seraphims, each one had six wings" (Isaiah 6:2).

The tower of the Russian Church of the Ascension (262) points to the sky from the Mount of Olives, a striking monument on the Jerusalem skyline. On a clear day it can even be seen from Jordan. The grounds, 832 metres above sea level, were purchased by the Russian Orthodox Church in 1870, and the building itself marks the site of the Ascension of Jesus. Two hundred and fourteen steps lead up six storeys to the top of the tower, but the view it commands of the whole of Jerusalem and its surroundings is well worth the climb. A huge bell, brought specially from Russia at great trouble and expense, hangs in the steeple.

During the construction, 5th-century and 6th-century Byzantine remains were revealed, among them mosaic floors bearing Armenian inscriptions. The Russians believe that in the south-eastern corner of the church lies the stone on which Mary stood with Jesus as he ascended to heaven.

258

259

260

The church now belongs to the Orthodox Palestine Society and the Russian Ecclesiastical Mission in Jerusalem, which is under the Synod of Bishops of the Russian Church outside Russia. Russian Orthodox nuns and, monks are familiar figures in Jerusalem.

In the last century the great influx of Russian Orthodox pilgrims to the Holy Land caused numerous hospices and hostels to be built for them in Jerusalem. In addition to the Russian Compound, which is located next to the Jaffa Road, hospices were built adjacent to the **Mary Magdalene Church** and the **Church of Ascension** on the Mount of Olives. Today, the former hospice buildings are used by the Russian nuns.

258. The Y.M.C.A. tower.
259/260. Architectural details of the Y.M.C.A. grounds.
261. The courtyard of the monastery in which live a few Russian nuns.
262. The Tower of Ascension in the Russian Compound.

261

262

263

Also set in Jerusalem's half-Mediterranean, half-desert landscape is the Anglican Cathedral and Tower of St. George (264). Were its stones damp and the sky grey, one might almost believe one were in Oxford. It was Bishop Blyth of Jerusalem who in 1888 purchased a plot of land not far from the Tombs of the Kings in what was then a solitary spot outside the Old City walls. His intention was to build an independent Anglican church, detaching the Anglicans for the first time from the Protestant and Lutheran institutions in the city. But Bishop Blyth also aimed to set up schools which were in great demand in Jerusalem at the time; a seminary for the study of biblical Hebrew as well as ancient Jewish philosophy in the appropriate surroundings; to found a centre for the study of the Eastern Churches, and a college for Anglican theologians.

The interior of the Cathedral, in romanesque-Gothic style, is typical of 19th-century Anglican churches, and is not unlike Christ's Church in the Old City. Named after England's patron saint who is believed to have been born and buried in Lydda, St. George's was consecrated in 1898. In the parvis stands a pillar discovered in the last century near

263. A courtyard window of the Church of St. George.
264. A view of the courtyard of St. George, with the Cathedral Tower.
265. Detail of one of the stained glass windows of the St. George Cathedral.
266. St. George's tower, with its four fairy-tale turrets, was erected in 1911 in memory of King Edward VII, but for fear of earthquakes it was not attached to the church. One cannot help regretting that its beauty is hidden from sight by a protective wall.

264

265

St. Stephen's Church (today's Dominican Ecole Biblique). Set on a Byzantine base, the pillar has a Corinthian capital, at the top of which is a delicately fashioned cross. Its origins are unkown.

St. George's Boys' School was opened in the same year as the Cathedral. One of the criteria for acceptance was that the boys would take the school's obligatory lessons in choral singing and become members of the Cathedral choir. Inevitably, all the pupils were Arab Christians, for the Moslems and Jews could not fulfil this requirement.

However, in the same year the St. George's Day School opened its doors and made the greatly sought-after English education available to all. A girls' school on the same lines as the Day School was founded in 1904 and functioned for ten years. The British Mandatory rule gave added impetus to the Church's activities, and during that time it succeeded in fulfilling all the aims of its founder. Its educational facilities were also developed, and opened to Jews and Moslems. In 1922 a pilgrims' hospice was built within the Cathedral's precincts, and in 1961 the Theological Seminary was reopened.

Bishop Blyth's ambitious project was motivated by the political and religious conditions prevailing in Jerusalem in the second half of the 19th century. The Protestants in Jerusalem had built a Cathedral and a hospital and a school had been built on Mt. Zion. Kaiser Wilhelm II asked Queen Victoria to agree to the establishment by the two countries of a joint Bishopric which would concentrate all Protestant activities in Jerusalem. The idea was accepted in principle by the British Cabinet, but it encountered opposition in the House of Lords, whose members did not consider that the Lutheran and Anglican creeds were identical on every question. Though an agreement was eventually reached, the association did not last long. One of the reasons for its collapse was the refusal of the Prussians to pay their share: they felt they were being discriminated against. In 1887, the Anglican Bishopric was established, a step which paved the way for the creation of the St. George complex.

After the dissolution of the agreement between the Lutherans and the Anglicans the Prussian Government backed their own churches now in the Holy Land. They established mission schools and churches all over the country. A good example is the new church which they built in the town of Bethlehem in the 1890's.

MARKETS AND BAZAARS

267

269

270

271

268

272

273

274

Ancient and modern, old and young, livestock and merchandise make up the colourful fabric of the city. Its rhythm is essentially unhurried, leisurely as a hookah or a donkey's quiet plodding. Buying and selling take up much of the time of young and old, men and women, natives and visitors. The markets are a feast for the eye and the nose, and shopping becomes a pleasure.

273. The entrance through Damascus Gate on the northern side of the Old City.
274. Solitary column with a Roman base in the Muristan Square in the bazaar.
275. The sheep-market near the northeastern corner of the city walls.
267-272/276. The dress of the inhabitants of Jerusalem is a colourful mixture of East and West. The red Ottoman tarboosh, Arab keffiyah and Jewish yarmulka are all familiar headgear in the city's streets. Transportation is equally varied, including mare's-

shank and the timeless donkey.
277-288. The brilliant array of goods displayed in the markets includes locally made items, such as Armenian ceramics, embroidered dresses, straw baskets, leather goods, sheepskin coats and the fragrant Kaïque bread, sprinkled with sesame seed. But there are imported items also — beaten brass and silverware from Iran, Damascus-made backgammon sets, French perfumes and Chinese and British carpets.

Colourful as a stage set for the Arabian Nights, the bazaars are a major attraction for the tourists.

275

276

277

279

281

282

283

284

285

286

287

288

WINDOWS AND ALLEYS

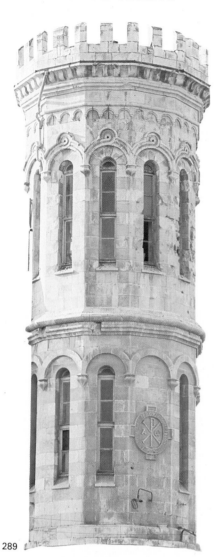

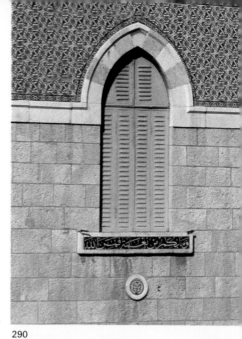

Like any other very old, continuously-inhabited city, Jerusalem combines a variety of styles — reflecting also, in this case, the cultures of the different communities that settled in it. The desert and mountain nature of the place made it impossible to decorate the city with parks or pleasure-grounds, which require plentiful water. The poverty of the inhabitants also left little opportunity for lavish display. The stone, natural substance of Jerusalem and its only resource, was worked in a dazzling variety of techniques — it is left rough, semi-smooth or polished like satin; it is carved in many elaborate styles; its subtle tones, from rose to creamy-white, are matched and contrasted.

289. A tower in the Russian Compound. 290-300. The many types of windows reflect the variety of architectural styles in the city. Wrought-iron grilles, potted plants and painted blinds enhance the rich texture of the stone walls.

290

289

291

292

293

294

295

296

297

298

299

300

A characteristic feature of Jerusalem architecture, one that recurs through the many styles and periods, are the twin windows. They appear in a rich variety of forms — topped with Gothic, Roman and Moorish arches, embellished with pillars and scrollwork in stone, demurely shuttered with rustic wooden blinds or richly filled with stained glass. The deep windowsills served generations of children as favourite seats, their sidelines view of the world.

301

302

303

301/303. A view of the arched windows of buildings near the Damascus Gate, erected at the beginning of this century.
302. The twin arched windows of the Beitar Building in the Jewish Quarter.
304. The windows of the Salome Jacir Frères School in Bethlehem.
305. The upper façade of one of the dormitory buildings beside the Anglican Christ church in the Old City of Jerusalem. This was the first church of its denomination to be established in the Middle East during the last century.
306/309. The house of Beit Thabor is situated on the Prophets' Street, in a beautiful old Jerusalem neighbourhood. It was built for his own residence by the nineteenth century architect and explorer Conrad Schick, whose discoveries helped to reveal the city's past history and glory.
307. The arched window of a house in the Bokharan Quarter in northern Jerusalem.
A large number of devout Jews from Bokhara settled in the Holy Land in the late nineteenth century.
308. A gothic-style window of the Italian Hospital, built during the First World War.
310. The Belloni Building in Bethlehem.
311. The Israeli Ministry of Health building formerly housed the Ottoman Health Ministry.
312. The Laemel School in new Jerusalem was named after the Austrian Jewish philanthropist Simon Von Laemel.
Built in 1890, it was one of the first Jewish schools outside the walls.

304

305

306

307

308

309

310

311

312

313

314

315

31

Stone lends itself naturally to archways as an engineering solution for openings, passages and buttresses.

In the Old City the narrow alleys are spanned by stone arches at regular intervals, providing shade as well as structural stability. Some of the stones have been used and reused since biblical times.

316

318

319

320

313/314. Alleyways in the Old City.
315. The arches of the Crusader Church in Bethany.
316. The passage leading to the Dormition Church Abbey on Mount Zion.
317. Beit-El Street in the Jewish Qtr.
318. A wall of windows and an arched passageway in the Old City.

319. A balcony in the Old City.
320. Jerusalem shops with their characteristic iron-doors.
321. The courtyard of Batei Mahseh in the Jewish Quarter.
322. The Khan El Sultan, built in the 14th century, served as a station house for travelling merchants.

321

322

323

324

325

In addition to the stone itself — hewn, polished and colour-matched — decorative touches were often added in the form of glazed tiles, bearing floral and geo-metrical designs, or commemorat-ive inscriptions; wrought-iron grilles for gates and windows, and ornate iron bosses on the doors.

The inscriptions often referred to the events associated with the construction of the building, the start of a new neighbourhood, the dedication of the premises as a synagogue, the name of the over-seas sponsors of the community, and so forth.

323. An inscription engraved upon the façade of the "Mishkenot Shaananim" building commemorating the donation of Judah Touro and the help of Sir Moses Montefiore in building the first Jewish habitation outside the walls of the Old City of Jerusalem, in the nineteenth century. The idea of establishing neighbourhoods outside the walls was, at that time, considered foolhardy because the land was ravaged by murderers, thieves and bandits. But the new settlement was the beginning of modern Jerusalem.
324. Adjacent to the Monastery of Mar-Elias, on the way to Bethlehem, is a bench commemorating the artist, William Holman-Hunt, who lived in Jerusalem in the nineteenth century. The Hebrew inscription is from the Second Book of Samuel 22:33: "God is my strength and power, and he maketh my way perfect."
325. A votive inscription commemorating a synagogue built in the "Ohel Moshe" Quarter of the city. The Quarter takes its name from Sir Moses Montefiore.
326. Ceramic plaques at the entrance to the New Gate of the Old City.
327. Stonework ornaments on a column.
328. Wrought-iron gate of a house.
329. A wrought-iron gate of the Armenian St. James Minor Church in the Armenian Quarter in the Old City.
330. A decorative iron door in the Christian Quarter.

326

327

328

329

330

"Judah is a lion's whelp: from the prey, my son, thou art gone up: he stooped down, he couched as a lion, and as an old lion; who shall rouse him up?" (Genesis 49:9.)

Although the lion has rarely been seen in the Land of Israel in historical times, its association with Zion recurs in many ways. *Ariel*, one of the many names of Jerusalem, also means lion. Many (not very realistic) representations of the royal beast decorate buildings in the city.

331. One of the twin lions decorating a gateway in the centre of Jerusalem, made by Rabbi Shlomo Simcha Janiver-Diskin, a well-known figure in Jerusalem in the late 19th, early 20th century.

332. A winged lion atop the "Generali Building" built by an Italian insurance company in 1931.

333. A mosaic depicting the Lion of Judah on the façade of the former Ethiopian Consulate building.

334. The twin lions of the Barclays Bank on Jaffa Road.

332

333

331　　　　　　334

At every turn and around every corner in Jerusalem the visitor is likely to stumble upon an unexpected work of art. In the basement of a building not far from Damascus Gate, between the Old City and the new, a magnificent mosaic floor (335) may be seen; it was uncovered only at the end of the 19th century when the foundations for the building were being laid. Known as the Armenian Mosaic, it is one of the most beautiful ever discovered in this country, and is the more impressive for having been preserved intact.

The floor is believed to have adorned the Armenian Church of St. Polyeucte, which stood in Jerusalem in Byzantine days. Armenian tradition tells that in the 3rd century Polyeucte, an officer of the Roman army, was executed for the crime of being a Christian, and the church was named after him. The mosaic bears an Armenian inscription which reads: "In memory and to the rescue of all Armenians, Our Lord knows their names." However, the late Professor Avi-Yonah was uncertain whether this was part of the original floor. He ascribed the mosaic to the "Gaza school," which in the 5th and 6th centuries produced many similar works. Examples of them have been revealed in the synagogues of Maon and Gaza, as well as in the churches of Shellal and Beit Guvrin.

335/336. The design of the Armenian Mosaic is made up of medallions and figures set facing each other. The central panel is decorated with bird, fruit and other motifs. At the bottom is an amphora flanked by peacocks.

335

336

338

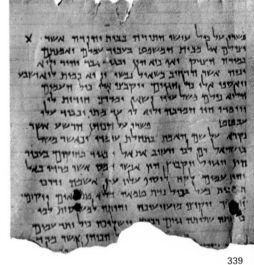

339

337

Close to Israel's Parliament, the Knesset, and near the Hebrew University Campus stand the buildings of the Israel Museum.

In the nineteen-fifties the Israel Government and the Jerusalem Municipality decided to build a museum to house the country's antiquities. In addition, there were to be wings for modern art and for folklore.

The museum, opened in 1965, has sections for archaeology, modern Jewish art, the Billy Rose Sculpture Garden (337; 338), the Shrine of the Book (340) and other sections.

The white dome of the Shrine of the Book and the black slab behind it signify the "War Between the Sons of Light and the Sons of Darkness," the subject of one of the Dead Sea Scrolls.

The interior of the structure is designed like a natural cave, with a tunnel leading to a round room over which is suspended the white dome. Along the tunnel and under the dome are displayed fragments of the scrolls which were discovered near the Dead Sea and in the Judaean desert between 1947 and the early 'sixties. Also

340

337/338. Statues in the Billy Rose Sculpture Garden of the Israel Museum.
339. Habakkuk's commentary from the Dead Sea Scrolls.
340. The Shrine of the Book.
341. A sarcophagus at the Rockefeller Museum.
342. A Roman altar at the Rockefeller Museum.
343. The façade of the Rockefeller Museum Building.

341

on display are artifacts found in the excavations with the scrolls.

The Dead Sea Scrolls illuminate the way of life and beliefs of Jewish sects during the turbulent period between the 2nd century B.C. and the 1st century A.D.

These scrolls and the region where they were found led some scholars to conclude that the writers, of the Essene sect, were forerunners of the first Christians.

Another interesting museum of antiquities is the Rockefeller Museum. It was built in the nineteen-thirties with the help of the Rockefeller family, and served as the headquarters for the Department of Antiquities in Palestine, and also as the country's principal museum during the British Man-

date. The museum served all of Palestine until 1948, and then until 1967 was run by the Jordanian Department of Antiquities. Since the June War of 1967 the museum has been managed by the Israel Department of Antiquities and today serves as its principal institution open to the public.

342

343

344

345

In the grounds of the Holy-Land Hotel in Jerusalem stands a model of the city in the Second Temple period, painstakingly reconstructed according to contemporary and recent discoveries. Built at the initiative of the late proprietor of the hotel, Mr. Kroch, the model was planned by the late Professor Avi Yonah, and is one of the most impressive of its kind. Not only does it provide the lovers of Jerusalem with a topographical view of the city; it also enables them to visualise the social, political and military aspects of life in ancient Jerusalem bringing such problems as the water supply and the city's defenses sharply into focus. Something of the architectural splendour of Herodian Jerusalem is reproduced by the use of the same building materials as were employed at the time.

The residential quarter of Mount Zion conveys a life-like impression of the architecture of the period, and of the ingenuity shown in exploiting to the maximum the limited area available. As for the Temple (334), the model illustrates the magnificence which made it famous. The biblical period is represented in the Siloam pool (348), frequently mentioned in the Bible and renowned to this day for the complicated engineering which its construction entailed (see page 96).

344. The model of the Second Temple at the Holy Land Hotel.
345. The view of the Lower City, with the Hippodrome in the background.
346. Private dwellings in the Upper City.
347. The Fortress of Antonia.
348. The Pool of Hezekia.

346

347   348

On a hilltop in the heart of the modern city of Jerusalem stands the Knesset, Israel's parliament. The building, a combination of classical and modern architecture, is set within the President's Park, and opposite the gate stands a large menorah (349), gift of the Jewish communities of Great Britain and Northern Ireland to the Knesset. On the seven branches of the candelabrum are depicted in relief the principal figures and events which marked the history of the Jewish people: the Patriarch Moses with the tablets of the law on Mount Sinai; Ruth the Moabite; David and Goliath; the prophet Isaiah and his vision of the End of Days; Jeremiah chastising the House of Israel; the Jews weeping for Zion by the rivers of Babylon; the reconstruction of Jerusalem by Nehemiah after the return of the exiles from Babylon; the wars of the Maccabees; Rabbi Yohanan ben Zakkai leaving Jerusalem for Yavneh; Hillel expounding the Torah; Bar Kokhba after the revolt; the Golden Age of the Jews of Spain; the Kabbala; the Warsaw Ghetto uprising; the modern return to the Land of Israel.

The memorial to John Fitzgerald Kennedy (350) in modern Jerusalem is built in the form of a felled tree, symbolising the President's life cut off in its prime. Each strip of the hollow glass and concrete construction bears the seal of one of the States of the United States of America.

349. The Menorah, donated by the Jewish communities of Great Britain, standing opposite the Knesset.
350. The Memorial to John F. Kennedy.

349

350

"Even unto them will I give in mine house and within my walls a place and a name ..." From this verse in the book of Isaiah (56:5) is taken the name *Yad Vashem*, the monument and memorial erected by the Jewish people to the six million Jews of Europe who perished in the Nazi holocaust. Beneath the dark basalt stones of the Hall of Memory, the ashes of the dead have been interred, and the sombre austerity of the chamber leaves a profound impression upon all who enter it (352/354). Below the Hall of Memory is the Museum of the Holocaust. In it are displayed documents and photographs showing the persecution of the Jews, and the conditions in which they lived — and died — in the death camps.

The approach to Yad Vashem is along a tree-lined way, the Allée des Justes. Each tree honours one of the "righteous gentiles" who risked, and sometimes gave their lives to save Jews.

Set among the rolling hills of Jerusalem, Yad Vashem symbolises the determination of the Jewish people never to forget. The very tranquility of the site inspires the hope that ultimately peace will come to this afflicted nation.

351. The sculptures which stand in the grounds of the memorial.
352/354. The entrance door and the wall of Yad Vashem memorial.
353. Jews being led to the concentration camps.

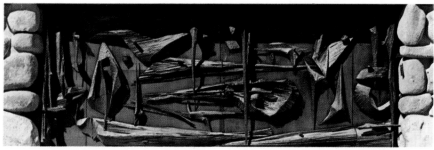

351

352

353

354

Index and Bibliography

Blyth, Estelle, "When We Lived in Jerusalem," London, 1927; Cressell, K.A.C., "Early Muslim Architecture," Vol. I, Parts, I, II, Oxford, 1969; Finn, J., "Stirring Times for Records from Jerusalem – Consular Chronicles of 1853–1856," Vol. I, London, 1878; Hamilton, R., "The Church of the Nativity, Bethlehem," Jerusalem, 1968; Hintlian, K., "History of the Armenians in the Holy Land," Jerusalem, 1976; Hoade, E., "Guide to the Holy Land," Jerusalem, 1976; Koriam, Y., "The Syrian Orthodox Church in the Holy Land," Jerusalem, 1976; Parkes, J., "A History of Palestine, from 135 A.D. to Modern Times," Oxford, 1949; Perowne, S., "The Pilgrim's Companion to Jerusalem and Bethlehem," Great Britain, 1964; Petrozzi, M., "Ain Karim," Jerusalem, 1971; "Bethlehem," Jerusalem, 1971; "Gethsemane," Jerusalem, 1972; Storme, A., "The Way of the Cross," Jerusalem, 1976; Van Berchem, M., "Matériaux Pour In Corpus Inscriptionum Arabicarum," (Deuxième Partie, Syrie du Sud) Tome Quarante-Troisième, Tome Premier, Jerusalem – Ville, Paris, 1922; Tome Quarante-Cinquième (Deuxième Partie, Syrie du Sud) Jérusalem, Paris, 1920; Van De Velde, C., "Narrative of a Journey Through Syria and Palestine in 1951 and 1952," Edinburgh, 1954; "Plan of the Town and Environs of Jerusalem," Gotha, 1858; Vilnay, Z., "Legends of Jerusalem," Philadelphia, 1975. ARTICLES (Alphabetical Order): Encyclopedia Judaica, Jerusalem, 1971; Kenaan, N., "Local Christian Art in Twelfth Century Jerusalem" (Part I), Israel Exploration Journal 23.3 (1973), pp. 176ff; (Part II), Israel Exploration Journal 23.4 (1973), pp. 221ff; Rahmani, Y., "The Eastern Lintel of the Holy Sepulchre," Israel Exploration Journal 26.2–3 (1976), pp. 120ff; Hough, W., "History of the British Consulate in Jerusalem," Journal of the Middle East Society 10–12 (1946); Schick, C., "Large Cistern Under the New Greek Building South-East of the Church of the Holy Sepulchre," Palestine Exploration Fund Quarterly Statement (1889), pp. 111ff; "Geographical Handbook Series/Palestine and Transjordan," London, 1939–45. HEBREW BIBLIOGRAPHY: Ben Zvi, I., "Eretz Israel Under Ottoman Rule for Centuries of History," 1955; Gat, B.Z., "The Jewish Community of Palestine in the Years 1840–1881," 1963; Vilnay, Z., "Jerusalem, Capital of Israel," 1970–1976. Vol. I The Old City, Vol. II The Old City & Environs, Vol. III The New City, Vol. IV The New City & Environs; Malachi, A.R., "Studies in the History of the Old Yishuv," 1971; Klausner, Y., "Jerusalem Past and Present," Odessa, 1914; Rivlin, A., "Jerusalem," 1966; Ben Arieh, Y., "A City Reflected in its Times," 1977. ARTICLES: Avi-Yonah, M., "The Gaza School of Mosaicists in the 5th–6th Centuries CE," Eretz Israel, Vol. XII (1975); Landau, Y.H., "Milestones Near Givat Jeshayahu," Yediot Bahaqirat Erets Israel Weatiqoteha, Vol. XXVIII (1964). In French: Benoit, P., "Découvertes archéologiques autour de la piscine de Béthesda," (in "Jerusalem Through the Ages" – Hebrew (1969)).

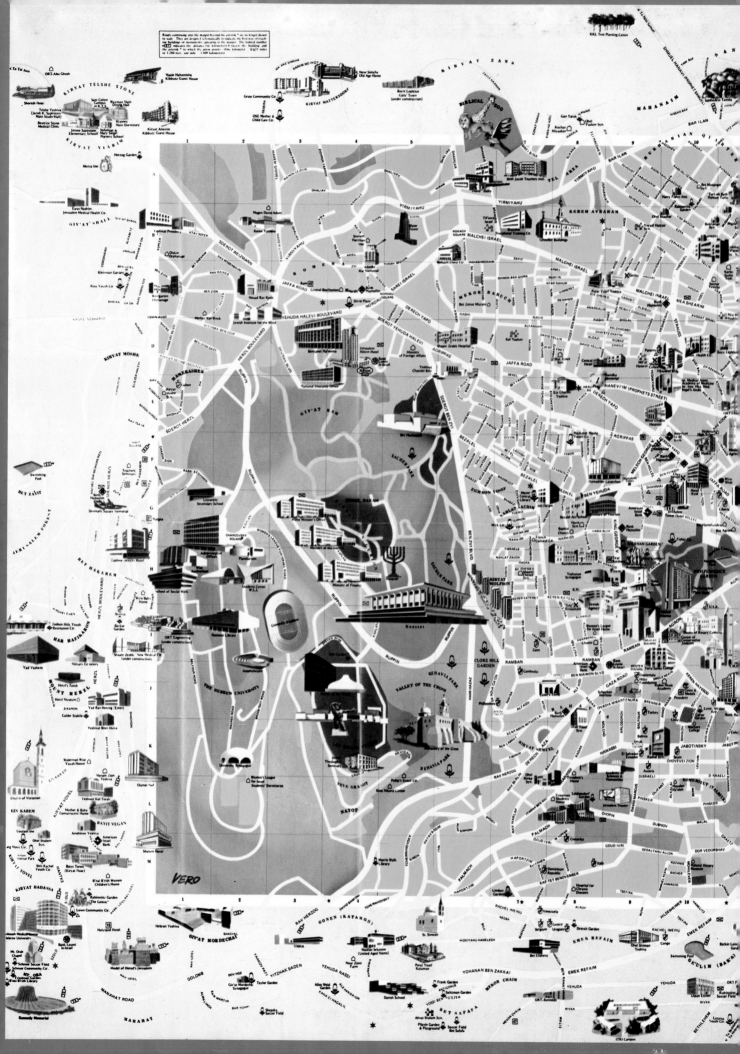